DUCT TAPE BAGS

40 Projects for Totes, Clutches, Messenger Bags, and Bowlers

Richela Fabian Morgan

Clarkson Potter/Publishers
New York

Copyright © 2016 by Richela Fabian Morgan
Principal photography © 2016 by Stephanie Gonot

All rights reserved.
Published in the United States by Clarkson Potter/Publishers, an imprint of
the Crown Publishing Group,
a division of Penguin Random House LLC, New York.
crownpublishing.com
clarksonpotter.com

CLARKSON POTTER is a trademark and POTTER with colophon is a
registered trademark of Penguin Random House LLC, New York.

Library of Congress Cataloging-in-Publication Data
Names: Morgan, Richela Fabian.
Title: Duct tape bags / by Richela Fabian Morgan.
Description: First edition. | New York : Clarkson Potter/Publishers, an imprint
of the Crown Publishing Group, a division of Penguin Random House LLC, [2016]
Identifiers: LCCN 2015027602 | ISBN 9780553448320 | ISBN 9780553448337
Subjects: LCSH: Handbags. | Tape craft. | Duct tape.
Classification: LCC TT667 .M665 2016 | DDC 745.59—dc23 LC record available at
http://lccn.loc.gov/2015027602

ISBN 978-0-553-44832-0
eBook ISBN 978-0-553-44833-7

Printed in China
Book design by Sonia Persad and Lauren Monchik
Jacket design by Jess Morphew and Sonia Persad
Jacket photography Stephanie Gonot

10 9 8 7 6 5 4 3 2 1

First Edition

For my mom and dad: I miss you every day.

And for Ed "GrandDad" Morgan

CONTENTS

THE BEAUTY OF DUCT TAPE

Bags are some of my favorite things. I feel that I should have the right to own as many of them as I want. Why? Because they make me happy.

To offset the cost of what can be an expensive collection, I make my own bags out of many materials. Because the closest fabric shop is at least a forty-minute drive from my house, I am more likely to search for raw materials in a grocery or hardware store. What I've discovered is that the most versatile material for making a bag is duct tape.

When duct tape is layered together into large double-sided pieces, it can be cut like cloth. But unlike traditional fiber-based material, this duct tape "fabric" does not need to be sewn with a needle and thread. The seams are held together with more duct tape, which means you won't be searching for the dreaded seam ripper after belatedly discovering a mistake.

The first time I made a duct tape fabric, I used black duct tape because it was a safe choice. Black matches everything, right? The fabric also resembled black patent leather, which I did not expect. After transforming it into a simple clutch bag, I was surprised by how little it resembled duct tape. It easily became my everyday purse. It wasn't long before I began trying out other colors and patterns of duct tape and making bags of various sizes and shapes.

Speaking of colors and patterns, you have so many offerings to choose from now: fabric-inspired options like chevron, plaid, argyle, linen, denim, leopard print, and camouflage. I've also seen tape named after wood: Brazilian rosewood, mahogany, and white oak.

Duct tape can be woven, striped, made into a faux patchwork, gathered into ruffles, or cut into fringes. It can be divided into pieces and fitted together like a jigsaw puzzle. It can be made into petals, which you can use like appliqué. All of this may sound as if it's delicate or intricate work, but the techniques in this book will show you how to do it all. You just need to remember that it's duct tape and almost any problem can be fixed. So don't be afraid to dive right in.

The information in the Essentials section that follows (page 6) contains a lot of the basics needed to complete each bag project. The most important thing to know is how to make a duct tape fabric (see page 10). Then you are ready to start crafting any style of bag.

You can undo something in the middle of a project to change a color or a shape. You can add more duct tape fabric if you belatedly discover that your measurements are wrong. You don't have to be intimidated; you can simply begin and play.

BASIC TOOLS OF THE TRADE

So what do duct tape crafters use besides duct tape and their massive arm strength? Here are lists of my must-haves and nice-to-haves.

Before diving headfirst into the colorful world of duct tape bags, you'll need to set up your crafting area with the right tools and materials. And it's also helpful to see how to actually make a duct tape fabric, which can be used for many things besides bags. Yes, you can buy a few rolls of duct tape and start crafting, but you can avoid wasting your materials by knowing the essentials beforehand.

YOU MUST HAVE

PARCHMENT PAPER (ALSO KNOWN AS BAKERY PAPER): this is not to be confused with traditional writing parchment, which is made from animal skin. Parchment paper is made with silicone and is nonstick. When making duct tape fabrics or duct tape stickers, strips of tape are placed on top of parchment paper and then later peeled off. Parchment paper is available at grocery stores; the standard roll size is 15" (38cm) wide.

SELF-HEALING CUTTING MAT, at least 18" × 24" (45.5cm × 61cm): duct tape will stay put but also will peel off with ease when placed on top of it.

SCISSORS, at least 6" (15cm) long: these are best for cutting strips off a roll or cutting down large duct tape fabrics into smaller pieces.

CRAFT KNIFE WITH EXTRA BLADES (size 11): use with a metal ruler to cut straight edges on duct tape fabrics.

METAL RULER WITH CORK BACK, 12" (30.5cm): use with a craft knife to make straight edges on the duct tape fabrics. The blade of the craft knife moves against the edge of the ruler as it cuts the fabric below it. The cork back prevents the ruler from moving.

GRAPHITE PENCIL: this is for tracing and drawing on top of parchment paper. Ink pens and markers will run, while the graphite of a pencil will adhere to the surface.

BALLPOINT PEN

GREASE PENCIL: also known as a China marker, this is for tracing a bag shape onto a duct tape fabric and making tick marks. It comes off easily with a little bit of oil.

FLAT-NOSE PLIERS: use to attach the store-bought closures to the bags.

HAMMER: use to attach the jeans button closure and the grommets to the bags.

DETAIL SCISSORS, spring-loaded with 3" (7.5cm) blade: these types of scissors are usually found in the floral-arrangement section of crafts stores or the gardening section of hardware stores. They are fantastic for cutting out intricate shapes.

OVERSIZE METAL RULER WITH CORK BACK, 24" (61cm) or longer: a bigger ruler makes cutting long lines easier, but it's not necessary.

STENCILS OF BASIC GEOMETRIC SHAPES (AND IN VARIOUS SIZES): although you can use cans or bottle caps to trace circles, stencils are more convenient.

CIRCLES INKING TEMPLATE, which is a stencil that can be found at arts and craft stores. They make tracing circles a lot easier and more accurate, sometimes down to the 32ndth of an inch.

⅛" (3MM) HOLE PUNCH: cutting out holes can be accomplished with scissors, but a hole punch can save time—and your hands.

KEEP YOUR METAL TOOLS CLEAN!

It is important to be sure all your metal cutting tools are well oiled and gunk-free. Before you start any cutting, rub a little oil on the blades with a paper towel or rag.

While you are crafting, be mindful of any gunk buildup on the blades and remove it before it causes a problem; when you are finished, be sure to clean and oil your tools.

You can use almost any oil or even petroleum jelly. Whenever I am crafting, I keep a paper towel with oil on it inside a nearby zip lock bag. If my scissors or craft knife starts to get gunky, then I dip them in the bag and wipe the blades on the paper towel. The gunk comes right off. I can zip up the bag and reuse the paper towel.

PLANNING AHEAD

TAPE USAGE

When dreaming up a bag, it's best to do a quick sketch to determine the parts. Of course

this is not necessary for the forty bag projects in this book because the dimensions and the parts are included. But once you decide to move outside the realm of this book, it's a good idea to carry a pencil and a small pad of paper with you; inspiration can happen at the strangest moments. Or, if you see a design, pattern, or even a bag that you like, don't be afraid to whip out your phone for a snapshot.

The type of bag you want should determine the size of the one you make. This will help you figure out how much duct tape you'll need. For instance, a wristlet or clutch is usually a small rectangular bag that is no larger than 10" (25.5cm) wide. If you are using a single color or patterned tape, you may need only one roll to complete your project. But a messenger bag, which is a larger rectangular bag that measures around 17" (43cm) wide and has a flap, may take three rolls of tape to complete. Make sure you have enough tape before starting your bag.

Here are some tips on gauging how much tape you'll need:

SMALL (maximum size is 8" wide × 8" high × 3" deep [20.5cm × 20.5cm × 7.5cm]): you will need at least 10 yd (9.1m) of duct tape.

MEDIUM (maximum size is 12" × 12" × 4" deep [30.5cm × 30.5cm × 10cm]): you will need 15–20 yd (13.7–18.2m) of duct tape.

LARGE (maximum size is 18" × 15" × 4" deep [45.5cm × 38cm x 10cm]): you will need at least 30 yd (27.4m) of duct tape.

The standard width of most duct tape rolls is 1.88" (4.78cm). Full rolls are available in 10 yd (9.1m), 15 yd (13.7m), 20 yd (18.2m), and 30 yd (27.3m). Silver, black, and white are usually available in 20 yd (18.2m) and 30 yd (27.3m) rolls. Other solid colors such as red, blue, or green are sold in 15 yd (13.7m) and 20 yd (18.2m) rolls. Patterns and prints come in 10 yd (9.1m) rolls. Be sure to read the yardage on the duct tape roll to make sure you get enough of the color, print, or pattern you want. For example, a 10 yd (9.1m) roll of duct tape is only enough for a small bag. So if you are looking to make a messenger bag with a patterned duct tape, one 10 yd (9.1m) roll may be enough for only the flap.

If you are making a small to medium bag, then one duct tape fabric will suffice. If you are making a large bag, you will need to make two fabrics and tape them together. While it is possible to make one oversize duct tape fabric, it is easier and more manageable to work with smaller fabrics. A larger duct tape fabric takes more time to complete. Smaller fabrics allow you to take a break from your project and not be completely lost when returning to it.

The color of the duct tape used for the fabric back side should not be an afterthought. The fabric's back side will eventually be the inside of the bag; a neutral print or solid color can give the impression that your bag is lined and give it an overall finished look.

After you finish some of the projects in this book, you can try to make one without a clear plan. Play around with the different methods used to create the designs in this book, such as weaving or pleating. Make a duct tape fabric just for the design aspect; treat the surface like a canvas and create colorful patterns of your own. Maybe then you'll be inspired to cut your fabric into a particular size or shape. Don't be afraid to let function take a backseat to your creativity.

PATTERNS AND TEMPLATES

In many projects, such as Regatta (page 95) and Galaxy (page 171), templates are provided for a design element or for the overall bag shape. For the bag-shape templates, cut along the outline and then place the template on top of the duct tape fabric. In many cases, the step-by-step instructions indicate that the template is for the left side and should be aligned with the left edges of the fabric or the parchment paper. You will need to flip the template or the parchment paper over for the mirror image and then complete the tracing, because the template is only giving you half of the actual bag shape or design element. Since most people—including myself—have printers that use letter-size paper, I tried to fit the template within the 8½" × 11" (21.5cm × 28cm) boundaries. If I was unable, I cut the template in half and gave instructions on how to use it.

For sticker templates, like the ones used in Caribbean Dream (page 133) and the Bowler Hat (page 115), you'll place a piece of parchment paper on top of them and then trace the template according to the step-by-step instructions. You'll stick duct tape over the parchment paper and flip it over; you'll still be able to see the tracing through the parchment paper because it is transparent. Cut the stickers out around the tracing and remove the parchment paper when indicated in the project instructions.

SECURING THE SEAMS

For securing the seams of your bags, it's best to use a heavy-duty duct tape. The stickier the tape, the better. However, the more industrial-strength stuff comes only in black, white, or the ubiquitous silver. If you are using a patterned or colored tape for the inside of the bag, set aside a few extra strips to cover up the heavy-duty tape used at the seams. To streamline the projects in this book, I've used only heavy-duty tape for the seams.

STORE-BOUGHT CLOSURES

There are three different types of store-bought closures in this book: a magnetic snap, a jeans button, and neodymium disc magnets. A magnetic snap is best used for messenger and flap bags, and a jeans button is the perfect closure for small bags. Neodymium disc magnets may sound impressive, but they are simple round magnets that you can pick up at any hardware store. They are cheap, readily available, and can be used on just about any type of bag.

HOW TO MAKE A DUCT TAPE FABRIC

TOOLS

- self-healing cutting mat
- parchment paper
- craft knife
- metal ruler with cork backing

Every project in this book requires at least one double-sided duct tape fabric. The instructions will start with the assumption that you already know how to make it. Please refer back to this tutorial as needed.

For the most part, you will always start with the back side of the fabric. The amount of duct tape required will be noted at the beginning of every project. When making the back side of the fabric, you will always need a piece of parchment paper. Strips are placed on top of the parchment paper, which makes it easier to turn the fabric and work on the other side. Ideally the size of the parchment paper should be the exact size of the fabric that you are making, which gives you a visual image of the size of the fabric you will need. The strips of tape you stick together to make the fabric should be approximately 1" (2.5cm) longer than the dimensions of the fabric, so the ends of each strip will stick to the cutting mat along the outer perimeter of the parchment paper. This prevents the whole fabric from moving until you are ready to flip it over.

BUBBLES. If there are bubbles in the fabric, puncture them to release the air and then run a finger over the bubble to smooth it out.

GAPS BETWEEN STRIPS. If the strips don't overlap properly and you see a gap, cover the gap with a narrow strip of tape that is the same color, print, or pattern.

STRIPS THAT ACCIDENTALLY GET STUCK IN THE WRONG PLACE. Cut off that offending strip as much as possible and then evaluate how much of the fabric was not affected. You can cut around it and then reattach the pieces with duct tape. Or you can cut out the salvaged piece and then build it back to the desired size by adding more strips.

1 Stick the first strip to the bottom edge of the parchment paper. //**A** Place the next strip above it on the parchment paper, overlapping the long edge approximately ⅛" (3mm) but no more than ¼" (6mm).//

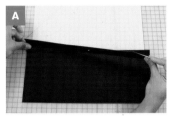

Repeat with the other strips, connecting them into one large piece. //**B** Once all the strips are on the parchment paper, the back side of the duct tape fabric is complete.//

2 //**C** Flip the working fabric over and gently remove the parchment: start at one of the bottom corners and pull up in a diagonal motion.// The sticky back of the tape will now be exposed. (Always save your parchment paper; it can be reused many times.)

3 **TO CREATE THE FRONT SIDE OF THE FABRIC,** start at one end and adhere the first strip to the back side of the fabric in the opposite direction so that it is perpendicular to the back strips; that is, if the back-side strips were placed in the horizontal position, then the strips for the front will be placed in the vertical position. This makes the fabric strong and less likely to tear.

//**D** Repeat, again overlapping the long edges of the strips approximately ⅛" (3mm) but no more than ¼" (6mm), connecting them into one large piece.//

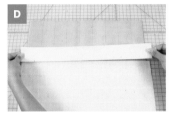

4 //**E** Using the metal ruler and craft knife, trim the fabric down to the desired size.// If you make a mistake in the middle of making the fabric, it is still possible to salvage all or some of it.

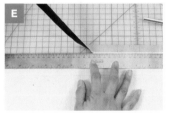

MAGNETIC SNAP CLOSURE

TOOLS

- self-healing cutting mat
- craft knife
- flat-nose pliers
- magnetic snap closure

All the magnetic snaps used in this bo ¾" (2cm) in diameter. Each one has a n a female part, and two washers. You wi pair of flat-nose pliers to fold down the the male and female parts. To maintain a front surface of the bag, it is best not to at male part directly to the bag fabric. Instea first attach it to a strip of duct tape and the on the inside of the bag.

1 //**A** Take the male part and push the 2 prongs against the center of your strip of tape.// (Each project will indicate the length of the tape strip you'll need.) Remove the male part to reveal 2 indentations made on the tape.

2 //**B** Using a craft knife make 2 small slits where the indentations are. Push the prongs of the male part through the slits.// The prongs should end up on the sticky side of the tape. Slip a washer through the prongs and use flat-nose pliers to fold the prongs down.

3 Place the strip of tape on the bottom edge and center it on the back side of the bag's flap.

4 Attach the female part to the male part. Close the flap and press down against the magnetic snap. The prongs of the female part should make indentations on the opposing side of the flap.

5 Open the flap. Use a craft knife to cut small slits where the prongs have made indentations. Push the prongs of the female part through the slits from the front side of the fabric. //**C** The prongs should end up on the inside of the bag.//

6 Slip a washer through the prongs and use a pair of pliers to fold the prongs down. Place a strip of tape over the washer to cover it.

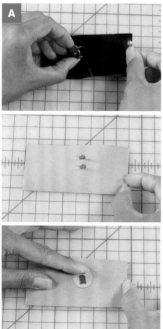

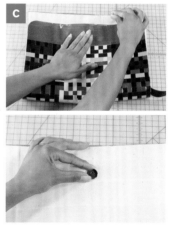

JEANS BUTTON CLOSURE

TOOLS

- self-healing cutting mat
- craft knife
- metal ruler with cork backing
- hammer
- jeans button

All the jeans buttons used in this book are ¾" (2cm) in diameter. A jeans button always comes with a metal brad that attaches to it from the back side of the duct tape fabric. You will need a hammer to attach this closure. Every project in this book that uses one will indicate the location for the jeans button.

1 **//A** Starting from the back side, push the brad through the duct tape fabric.**//** The brad is very sharp and should easily pierce the fabric

//B Place the jeans button on top of the brad.**//** Firmly but gently tap on the top of the jeans button with a hammer until it is attached to the brad.

2 On the flap of the bag, use a craft knife to cut a 1" (2.5cm) horizontal slit. Cut that slit into an elongated spheroid (football shape) approximately ⅛" (3mm) high for the buttonhole.

3 Close the flap over the jeans button. Push the jeans button through the slit to finish the closure.

NEODYMIUM MAGNET CLOSURE

TOOLS

- self-healing cutting mat
- neodymium magnets

All the neodymium magnets used in this book are ½" (13mm) in diameter and 1⁄16" (1.5mm) thick. Every closure will need at least one pair of magnets and two strips of heavy-duty duct tape. Each project will state how long the tape strips need to be. If the project calls for two pairs of magnets, be sure that they are positioned 1" (2.5cm) from the outer ends of the tape strips.

1 Place the first duct tape strip lengthwise on the worktable, sticky side facing up.

2 **//A** Stick the magnet or first pair of magnets to the strip of duct tape.**//** Flip over the strip of tape so the sticky side is facing down.

3 **//B** Place the second strip, sticky side facing up, directly on top of the first strip.**//** Be sure to line up the edges.

4 **//C** Stick the second magnet or pair of magnets to the second strip.**//** Allow it to be attracted to the first magnet or pair of magnets below the tape strips.

5 Place the magnets or tape strip on opposing bag edges. **//D** Make sure the magnets are in the correct location in order for them to attach to the opposite set and close the bag opening properly.**//**

CLUTCH & WRISTLET

I'm a firm believer that good things come in small packages—or I should say small bags. Clutches and wristlets may seem like trifles in the big, bad world of oversize carryalls, but they can be the awesome accessories that tie an outfit together.

For traveling light, nothing beats a clutch, because it forces you to take only what you need. And for a night on the town, a wristlet provides the compactness of a clutch, but with the added strap to loop around your hand, so the chance of misplacing it is slim.

SUMMER FLING

When I see this little sky-blue wristlet, I imagine myself strolling along the boardwalk in a sundress and strappy sandals. It dangles from my wrist, securely containing life's necessities: a few dollars for ice cream, my sunglasses, and a tube of coconut-scented sunblock. And just like a beach bum, the Summer Fling is a little lazy, a bit flirty, and entirely focused on having fun.

DUCT TAPE
white (heavy duty), 3 yd (2.7m)
light blue, 3 yd (2.7m)
white (regular), 1 yd (0.9m)

ADDITIONAL MATERIALS
parchment paper, 13½" × 10"
 (34.5cm × 25.5cm)
magnetic snap closure, ¾" (2cm)
 diameter

TOOLS
• scissors
• craft knife
• metal ruler
• white grease pencil
• flat-nose pliers

1 Place the parchment paper on the worktable in the portrait position. Make a duct tape fabric (see page 10) for the back side using 8 strips of 11" (28cm) white heavy-duty duct tape. Flip the working fabric over so the parchment paper is facing up. Trim the fabric to 13½" × 10" (34.5cm × 25.5cm). Gently peel off the parchment paper, exposing the sticky side of the fabric. Set aside.

2 **TO MAKE THE PLEATS FOR THE FRONT OF THE BAG,** place 6 strips of 14½" (37cm) light blue duct tape on the worktable with the sticky sides facing up.

//**A** On each strip, fold back one of the long edges approximately ⅛" (3mm).//

3 You will now add the pleats to the sticky side of the fabric, perpendicular to the direction of the strips on the back side. Line up the folded edge of the first pleat with the outer left edge of fabric. Add the next pleat so that it overlaps the first pleat by about ⅛" (3mm),

again with the folded edge on the left side. Repeat with a third pleat. Starting at the outer right edge of the fabric, line up the folded side of a pleat so that the folded edge is on the right. Repeat with the other 2 pleats. //**B** There should be a space in the center of the 3 pleats on the right and the 3 on the left.//

4 **TO MAKE THE WHITE PLEAT** that goes in the center, cut a 14½" (37cm) strip of white regular duct tape. Fold back both long edges approximately ⅛" (3mm). **//C** Place the pleat in the center of the blue pleats, covering the open space.//

5 Trim the height of the fabric to 13½" (34.5cm). Flip the fabric over so the white heavy-duty side is facing up. Be sure it's in the portrait position.

6 Starting at the bottom corners, measure up 4¾" (12cm) along the left and right edges. Mark these points with a grease pencil.

7 Carefully cut a 4¾" (12cm) strip of white heavy-duty duct tape in half lengthwise. **//D** Starting at the bottom corners, place a strip vertically on both the left and right edges of the fabric. Be sure that only half of each strip is on the fabric so you can fold the strips back.//

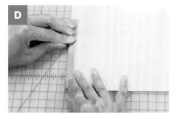

8 **//E** As you fold back the tape strips along the left and right edges, pull up the bottom edge of the fabric so it folds horizontally at the 4¾" (12cm) marks.// The sticky side of the tape strips should close up the side seams, creating a pouch with a top flap.

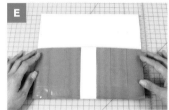

9 To flatten the bottom of the bag, measure ½" (13mm) inward from each corner along the bottom edge. **//F** Mark these points with a grease pencil.//

10 Cut a 3½" (9cm) strip of blue duct tape in half lengthwise. **//G** Pinch each bottom corner of the bag into a triangle. Fold the point of the triangle down and inward along the bottom of the bag, making a perpendicular line at the ½" (13mm) mark.//

Attach the strips of blue duct tape across the tip of the corner triangle and against the bag to hold them in place.

11 **TO MAKE THE STRAP, //H** fold a 14" (35.5cm) strip of white regular tape lengthwise into thirds, then fold it in half crosswise. Insert 3" (7.5cm) of the open end of the strap inside the left corner of the bag opening at a 45-degree angle.//

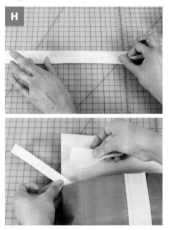

Place a 4" (10cm) strip of white heavy-duty duct tape over the open strap end, attaching it to the inside of the bag.

12 Trim the corners of the flap in a curved line, rounding them.

13 Use 2 strips of 3" (7.5cm) white heavy-duty duct tape to center and attach the magnetic snap closure (see page 12) ½" (13mm) from the edge of the flap.

OPERA

Opera is a classic little purse that every woman should have in her collection. Opera also can be *the* accessory, the sassy piece of your ensemble. If you're not altogether sure how to jazz up your style for the evening, pair your outfit with this shiny gold clutch. It also makes any gold jewelry that you are wearing pop.

DUCT TAPE
black (heavy duty), 5 yd (4.6m)
gold chrome, 5 yd (4.6m)

ADDITIONAL MATERIALS
parchment paper, 12" × 12" (30.5cm × 30.5cm)
printout of template for bag lips (see page 198), trimmed to outline of shape
empty ½-gallon (1.89L) milk carton, rinsed, dried, and taken apart at the seams
2 neodymium magnets, ½" (13mm) diameter, ¹⁄₁₆" (1.5mm) thick

TOOLS
• scissors
• craft knife
• metal ruler
• white grease pencil

1 Place the parchment paper on the worktable. Make a duct tape fabric (see page 10) using 8 strips of 13" (33cm) black duct tape for the back side and 8 strips of 13" (33cm) gold duct tape for the front side. Trim the fabric to 12" × 12" (30.5cm × 30.5cm).

2 Place the fabric with the black side facing up. Measure up 6" (15cm) from the bottom corners along the left and right edges. Mark with a grease pencil.

3 Carefully cut a 6" (15cm) strip of black duct tape in half lengthwise. //**A** Starting at the top corners of the fabric, vertically add a strip to both the left and right edges of the fabric, placing only half of each strip lengthwise on the fabric so you can fold the strips back.//

As you fold back the tape strips along the left and right edges, //**B** pull up the bottom edge of the fabric so it folds horizontally at the middle. Line up the left and right edges of the fabric, and press down the folded tape strips to secure the seams.//

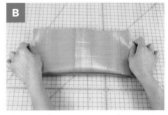

4 From each of the bottom corners, measure 1½" (3.8cm) inward along the bottom edge and measure up 1½" (3.8cm) along the left and right edges. **//C** Mark these four spots with a grease pencil.**//**

5 Push in each bottom corner until a diagonal line forms between the 1½" (3.8cm) marks. **//D** Cover each inverted corner with a 2" (5cm) strip of gold duct tape. Starting at the top of one side seam, center a 4½" (11.5cm) strip of gold duct tape down the side of the bag to cover the seam.**//** Repeat on the other side. Set aside.

6 **TO MAKE THE BAG LIPS,** place the template on top of the milk carton. **//E** Using a grease pencil, trace it twice. Cut out both shapes from the milk carton.**//**

7 Place one lip in the center of a 12" (30.5cm) strip of gold duct tape so that it completely covers the lip. **//F** As you cover it, make uneven wrinkles on the surface of the tape.**//**

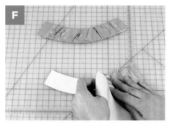

Flip it over and fold any extra tape over the edges. Repeat with the other lip.

8 Cut 12 strips of 1" (2.5cm) black duct tape. **//G** On one side of the bag, make 6 vertical folds along the top edge opening that are each approximately ¼"–½" (6mm–13mm), spacing the folds as evenly as possible.**//** Repeat on the other side of the bag.

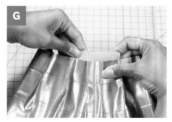

//H Use the 1" (2.5cm) black duct tape strips to hold the folds in place on the inside.**//**

This should reduce the width of the opening to approximately 8" (20.5cm). (There is some wiggle room since the bag lips are curved.)

9 Position the bag on the worktable so the opening is at the top edge. **//I** Place a bag lip on top of the bag opening so that the lip covers it.**//**

Cut 8 strips of 1" (2.5cm) black duct tape. Place these strips on the inside of the bag where the lip and the top edge of the bag meet, connecting them. Flip the bag over, cut another 8 strips of 1" (2.5cm) black duct tape, and repeat with the other lip.

10 Using 2 strips of 3" (7.5cm) black duct tape, create a neodymium magnet closure (see page 14). Attach the neodymium magnets to the back side of the lips.

DCC
FRINGE

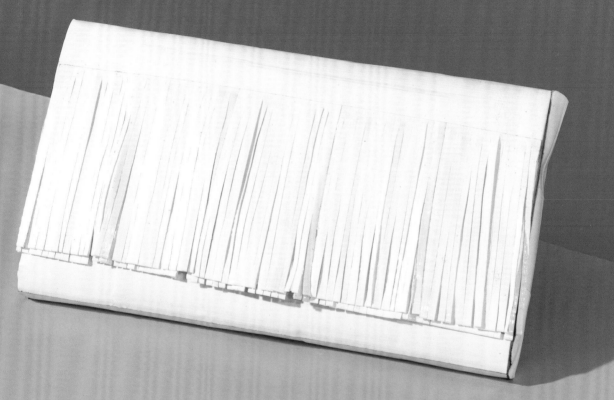

I admit it: when I was a little girl, I wanted to be a Dallas Cowboys cheerleader. No, I didn't watch a lot of football. In fact, to this day I know nothing about the rules and regulations of the game. But during my childhood, it seemed like the Dallas Cowboys were always in the Super Bowl—and who didn't watch the Super Bowl?

This bag is an homage to the famed cheerleading squad. While carrying this clutch around, you can pretend it's a white, fluffy pom-pom and practice your ultimate cheer.

DUCT TAPE

black (heavy duty), 4 yd (3.7m)
white, 6 yd (5.5m)

ADDITIONAL MATERIALS

parchment paper, 10" × 15½"
   (25.5cm × 39.5cm)
magnetic snap closure, ¾"
   (2cm) diameter

TOOLS

• scissors
• craft knife
• metal ruler
• white grease pencil
• flat-nose pliers

1 Place the parchment paper on the worktable in the landscape position and make a duct tape fabric (see page 10) using 6 strips of 16½" (42cm) black duct tape for the back side and 9 strips of 11" (28cm) white duct tape for the front side. Trim the fabric to 10" × 15½" (25.5cm × 39.5cm).

2 **TO MAKE THE SIDES OF THE BAG,** trim off a piece that measures 1" × 15½" (2.5cm × 39.5cm) from the fabric. Set aside the main fabric, which is now 9" × 15½" (23cm × 39.5cm). Cut the narrow piece into 2 pieces that measure 1" × 5" (2.5cm × 12.5cm) each. Discard the extra fabric.

3 Round one end of a bag side by cutting the corners in a curved line. Leave the other end intact. Repeat with the other bag side.

4 Place the main fabric on the worktable in the portrait position with the black back side facing up. //A Place a bag side vertically along both the left and right edges of the main bag fabric, black sides facing up, and line up the straight bottom edges.//

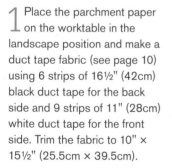

5 Cut an 11" (28cm) strip of black duct tape in half lengthwise. //B Connect the bag sides to the main fabric by covering the seam between them with the tape, starting at the bottom edge and working your way up. (The tape will extend above the side of the bag.)//

//C Starting at the bottom, pull up the fabric so the left and right edges touch the rounded end of the bag sides.//

//D While doing so, be sure to press the sticky tape strip against the inside of the main fabric and the bag sides to hold them in place.// Repeat on the other side.

6 TO MAKE THE BAG'S FRINGES, place 10 strips of 7½" (19cm) white duct tape on the worktable lengthwise, nonsticky white side facing up. Starting from the top edge, measure down and mark 4" (10cm) on each strip. //E Fold up each strip at the 4" (10cm) mark, sticky sides together. A

½" (13mm) sticky section will remain exposed on each strip.//

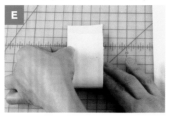

7 Rotate each folded strip so the folded end is along the bottom edge and the sticky section is at the top. //F From the bottom, cut 2" (5cm) vertical slits into the strips, making approximately 10–15 slits per strip.//

8 Place the bag on the worktable so the flap is open and the inside of the bag is facing the worktable; the flap should also be positioned at the bottom. From the bottom corners of the flap, measure up 3¾" (9.5cm) on the left and right edges and mark these points with a grease pencil. Lightly draw a horizontal line connecting the marks.
//G Stick 5 fringe strips to the flap, aligning the sticky edges with the horizontal line. (The fringed edge is at the bottom.)//

Trim any excess at the left and right edges of the flap. This is the first row of fringes. //H Repeat this step with the remaining 5 fringe strips for the second row, placing them about ⅛" (3mm) above the first row.//

9 //I Cover about ½" (13mm) of the top edge of the top row horizontally with a 9" (23cm) strip of white duct tape.//

10 Use 2 strips of 4" (10cm) black duct tape to center and attach the magnetic snap closure ½" (13mm) from the edge of the flap (see page 12).

SUGAR MAMA

Sugar Mama is the perfect oversize clutch that holds all of your important things without being cumbersome. With its sleek silhouette, no one will suspect that an electronic tablet or mini laptop is inside. The dark green and blue chevron pleats are neatly brought together with a central gold band, adding the right touch of vivacity to an otherwise verdant palette. Carrying it can make you stand or walk a little more sexy and confident.

DUCT TAPE
white (heavy duty), 7 yd (6.4m)
dark green, 9 yd (8.2m)
blue chevron, 3 yd (2.7m)
gold chrome, 1 yd (0.9m)

ADDITIONAL MATERIALS
parchment paper, 14½" × 16" (37cm × 40.5cm)
4 neodymium magnets, ½" (13mm) diameter, ¹⁄₁₆" (1.5mm) thick

TOOLS
• scissors
• craft knife
• metal ruler
• white grease pencil

1 Place the parchment paper on the worktable in the portrait position. Make the back side of a duct tape fabric (see page 10) using 10 strips of 15½" (39.5cm) white duct tape. After completing the back side, flip the working fabric over so the parchment paper is facing up. Trim the fabric to 14½" × 16" (37cm × 40.5cm). Gently peel off the parchment paper, exposing the sticky side. Be sure the working fabric is still in the portrait position. Set aside.

2 **TO MAKE THE PLEATS,** place 14 strips of 17" (43cm) dark green duct tape and 4 strips of 17" (43cm) blue chevron duct tape on the work surface with the sticky sides facing up. //A Fold back approximately ¼" (6mm) of one long edge on each strip.//

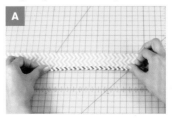

3 Flip over a dark green pleat so the sticky side is facing down. Align its folded long edge with the left edge of the unfinished fabric and stick it down. Be sure that it is perpendicular to the direction of the strips on the back side. Working from the left to the right, repeat with 2 more dark green pleats, overlapping the long edges approximately ¾" (2cm). Continuing to work from left to right, attach the following pleats in the same manner, all

overlapping approximately ¾" (2cm) at the long edges: blue chevron, 3 more dark green, then 1 blue chevron, and finally another dark green. The folded long edges of the pleats should always be on the left.

4 Repeat step 3 on the right edge of the unfinished fabric with the remaining pleats in the same order, but going from right to left; the folded long edges of the pleats should always be on the right. When you are done, there should be an open space in the middle of the fabric approximately ½" (13mm) wide.

5 **TO MAKE THE GOLD PLEAT,** fold back both long edges of a 17" (43cm) strip of gold duct tape approximately ¼" (6mm). **//B** Place this pleat in the center of the fabric, covering the open space.**//**

6 The fabric should be 14½" (37cm) wide; trim the height to 16" (40.5cm). The fabric is complete. Flip the fabric over so the white back side is facing up and set it aside.

7 **TO MAKE A SECOND FABRIC,** use 4 white (for the back side) and 4 dark green (for the front side) 15½" (39.5cm) strips. (Because this is a small fabric, the direction of the strips on the front and back sides can be the same.) Trim it down to 14½" × 4½" (37cm × 11.5cm). From this small fabric, cut a 14½" × 3½" (37cm × 9cm) piece and set it aside. (This will be used in step 14.)

8 **TO MAKE THE SIDES OF THE BAG,** from the remaining fabric from step 7 cut 2 strips that measure 6" × 1" (15cm × 2.5cm) each. Discard the extra piece.

9 **//C** Place a bag side vertically along the left and right edges of the fabric, white sides facing up, so they touch and create a seam. Line up the bottom edges.**//**

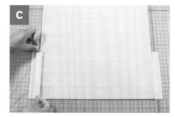

Cut a 6" (15cm) strip of white tape in half lengthwise. **//D** To connect the sides to the fabric, place a white duct tape strip vertically over the seams between each bag side and the main fabric.**//**

10 Pull up the bag fabric from the bottom edge so the bottom 6" (15cm) portion of the fabric is standing perpendicular to the worktable, with the bag sides attached to it. Pull the bottom edges of the bag sides so each touches the outer edge of the main fabric. Cut 2 strips of 1" (2.5cm) white duct tape. **//E** Place a strip along the bottom edge of each bag side so it sticks to the back side of the main bag fabric.**//**

11 Fold the bottom of the bag fabric so the remaining unattached edges of the bag sides touch the main bag fabric and create a seam. Cut a 6" (15cm) strip of white heavy-duty tape in half lengthwise. **//F** To connect the sides to the fabric, place a white duct tape strip over the seam between each bag side and the main bag fabric.**//**

12 **TO MAKE THE FLAP EXTENSION,** place the bag on the worktable with the flap open and facing up. **//G** Place the small fabric from step 7 above the bag in the landscape position, white side facing up and edges touching to create a seam.**//**

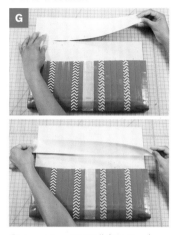

Cut a strip of 15½" (39.5cm) white duct tape. Place it horizontally over the seam between the bottom edge of the flap extension and the top edge of the bag flap. Trim off any excess tape.

13 Flip the bag over. Fold back both long edges of a 17" (43cm) gold chrome strip approximately ¼" (6mm). **//H** Place it horizontally over the seam between the flap and the flap extension.**//** Trim off any excess tape.

14 With a pair of scissors, cut the corners off the flap in a curved line, rounding them.

15 Attach the 4 neodymium magnets to 2 strips of 8" (20.5cm) white duct tape, 2 magnets per strip (see page

14). Centrally place one strip on the bottom edge of the inside of the flap. Place the second strip on top of the first strip, nonsticky sides facing each other. Make sure the magnets are in the correct location to attach to the opposite set.

16 Close the bag flap. The second strip should attach to the opposing side of the flap. Open the flap. Cover the white tape strip with 2 strips of 9" (23cm) dark green duct tape.

SUNDANCE KID

When we hear "red paisley," we think of bandanas. While they themselves aren't the most stylish of accessories, that bandana print has somehow made its way into modern fashion in the form of dresses, shirts, and skirts. This ruffled bandana wristlet, with a name alluding to an icon of the Wild West, is fittingly matched with a pair of cowboy boots and a denim dress—and maybe even a ten-gallon hat.

DUCT TAPE
white (heavy duty), 4 yd (3.7m)
red bandana, 10 yd (9.1m)

ADDITIONAL MATERIALS
parchment paper, 10½" × 11½"
    (26.5cm × 29cm)
4 neodymium magnets, ½" (13mm) diameter,
    ¹⁄₁₆" (1.5mm) thick

TOOLS
• scissors
• craft knife
• metal ruler
• white grease pencil

1 Place the parchment paper on the worktable in the landscape position and make a duct tape fabric (see page 10) using 7 strips of 12½" (32cm) white duct tape for the back side and 7 strips of 11½" (29cm) red bandana duct tape for the front side. Trim the fabric to 10½" × 11½" (26.5cm × 29cm). Set aside.

2 Place a 15" (38cm) red bandana duct tape strip on the worktable with the sticky side facing up. Fold back one long edge approximately ¼"

(6mm). //A Place another 15" (38cm) red bandana duct tape strip on top of it with the sticky side facing down. Be sure to align the long edge of the top strip with the folded long edge of the bottom strip.// You should now have a double-sided strip with a ¼" (6mm) wide sticky section on the back side.

3 Repeat step 2 five more times to make a total of 6 double-sided strips. These will be used for the ruffles on the front side of the fabric. Set aside.

4 Flip the main fabric over so the red bandana side is facing up. Place it in the portrait position.

5 From the bottom corners, measure up 1½" (3.8cm) along the left and right edges. Mark these points with a grease pencil and draw a horizontal

line across the fabric to connect them. Measure up 3" (7.5cm) from this line on the left and right sides of the fabric. Mark these points and draw another horizontal line between them. From the top corners of the fabric, measure down 1½" (3.8cm) on the right and left edges. Mark these points and draw a horizontal line between them. Then measure down 3" (7.5cm) from the 1½" (3.8cm) line on both edges, mark, and draw a horizontal line between them.

6 Measure 2¼" (5.5cm) from the left corner across the top edge of the fabric and mark it with a grease pencil. From that point, measure 2" (5cm), then 2" (5cm), and another 2" (5cm). //B From those points, carefully and lightly draw vertical lines with a grease pencil down the fabric, creating a grid.//

7 Take a strip from steps 2 and 3 and hold it horizontally with the sticky side facing down and the folded edge along the bottom. Place the right end of the strip at the 3" (7.5cm) line on the right edge of the fabric and fold approximately ½"

(13mm) under the right side edge of the bag/main fabric. Carefully attach the strip to the 3" (7.5cm) horizontal line across the fabric, working your way from right to left and pressing the top edge to align with the grease-pencil line. When you reach the first vertical line, vertically pleat the strip ¼" (6mm) (total fold takes up ½" [13mm]) so the fold is facing left. Continue attaching the strip until you get to the second vertical line. Vertically pleat the strip ¼" (6mm) again, but this time the fold should face right. Continue attaching the strip until you get to the third vertical line, then vertically pleat the strip ¼" (6mm) so the fold is facing left. Continue attaching the strip until you reach the fourth and last vertical line. //C Vertically pleat the strip ¼" (6mm) one last time, with the fold facing right.//

Finish attaching the strip along the horizontal line, and fold any excess part of the strip over the left edge of the fabric.

8 Using another strip from steps 2 and 3, repeat step 7 on the horizontal line 1½" (3.8cm) from the top edge of the fabric.

9 Using another strip from steps 2 and 3, repeat step 7 on the top edge of the fabric. Cut a 10½" (26.5cm) strip of red bandana duct tape and fold ½" (13mm) to the inside/ back side. This should cover the top edge of the last ruffle and secure it to the fabric.

10 Rotate the fabric on the worktable 180 degrees. //D Repeat steps 7–9 with the remaining strips from step 3.//

When all the ruffles are attached, flip the fabric over so the white back side is facing up. Keep the fabric in the portrait position.

11 TO MAKE THE STRAP, fold a 14" (35.5cm) strip of red bandana tape lengthwise into thirds, then fold it in half crosswise.

12 To attach the strap, you'll need two 2" (5cm) strips of white duct tape. //E Starting at the top corners of the fabric, place a strip on each of the outer edges so that only half of each strip is on the fabric lengthwise. Pull back the top left corner of the left white duct tape strip. Hold the strap from step 11 at a 45-degree angle

and place approximately 2" (5cm) of one end at the top left corner of the fabric.//

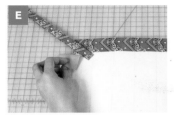

//**F** Replace the top of the white duct tape strip, covering part of the strap end.//

//**G** Fold the left side of the white duct tape strip in half lengthwise so that the sticky side is facing up.//

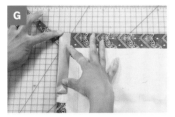

//**H** Fold the strap in half and stick the other end to the top, sticky side of the tape strip.//

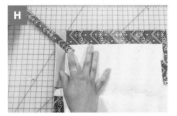

//**I** Pull up the bottom edge of the fabric and fold it in half, matching the top edges.//

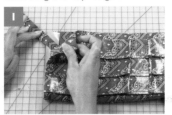

Line up the left edge and push the fabric down against the folded tape strip. The left seam and bag strap are now secure.

13 Fold the white duct tape strip on the right side in half lengthwise so that half of the sticky side is now facing up. Pull the bottom right corner of the fabric up to meet the top right corner. //**J** Line up the right edge of the fabric and push it down against the folded strip.// The right seam is now secure. The main bag is complete.

14 From each of the bottom corners, measure ½" (13mm) inward along the bottom edge and mark with a grease pencil.

15 To flatten the bottom of the bag, cut a 9" (23cm) strip of red bandana duct tape. Pinch each bottom corner of the bag into a triangle. //**K** Fold the point of the triangle down and inward along the bottom of the bag, making a perpendicular line at the ½" (13mm) mark.//

Place the red bandana duct tape strip across the bottom of the bag. This should hold the folded corners in place.

16 //**L** With 2 strips of 8" (20.5cm) white tape, attach the 4 neodymium magnets to the opposite sides of the bag opening (see page 14); there should be 2 magnets on each side.// Place a magnet approximately 1" (2.5cm) from the edge.

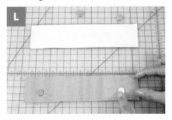

THE MATRIX

This clutch has a futuristic patchwork on the flap. The grid of multicolored triangles transforms a plain bag into a diverting one. It's a kaleidoscope of colors that almost seems to twinkle, and you can discern a pattern if you really try. Despite its appearance, this is an easy bag to make, and these basic instructions can be mastered for future bag projects. Before you know it, you'll be engineering the flap design yourself.

DUCT TAPE
white (heavy duty), 5 yd (4.6m)
dark blue, 4 yd (3.7m)
gold chrome, 1 yd (0.9m)
pastel pink, 1 yd (0.9m)
purple, 1 yd (0.9m)
burgundy, 1 yd (0.9m)

ADDITIONAL MATERIALS
parchment paper, 11" × 18"
   (28cm × 45.5cm)
2 neodymium magnets, ½" (13mm)
   diameter, ¹⁄₁₆" (1.5mm) thick

TOOLS
• scissors
• craft knife
• metal ruler
• white grease pencil

1 Place the parchment paper on the worktable in a portrait position and make a duct tape fabric (see page 10) using 11 strips of 12" (30.5cm) white duct tape for the back side and 7 strips of 19" (48.5cm) blue duct tape for the front side. Trim to an 11" × 18" (28cm × 45.5cm) fabric.

2 **TO MAKE THE SIDES OF THE BAG**: //A Trim off a piece from the fabric that measures 2" × 18" (5cm × 45.5cm).//
Set aside the main fabric, which now is 9" × 18" (23cm ×

45.5cm). Cut the narrow piece into 2 pieces that measure 2" × 5½" (5cm × 14cm) each. Discard the extra fabric.

3 **ATTACH SIDES:** Place the fabric on the worktable in the portrait position, white side facing up. Place a bag side vertically along the left

and right edges of the fabric, white side facing up, so they touch and create a seam. Line up the bottom edges. Cut a 5½" (14cm) strip of white duct tape in half lengthwise. //B To connect the sides to the fabric, place a halved 5½" (14cm) white duct tape strip over the seam between each bag side and the fabric.//

4 Cut 2 strips of 2" (5cm) white heavy-duty duct tape. Place a strip lengthwise over each bottom edge of the bag sides. Be sure that only half of the strips are on the fabric

VENUS

This bag is a high-art mash-up: Botticelli's *The Birth of Venus* meets the Art Deco style of the 1920s. This clutch is all about the clamshell in its gold-and-silver glory. It is an accessory that feels right at home whether the setting is a museum gala or a Parisian nightclub. I imagine wearing a mermaid evening gown with this clutch. It would be a nautical ensemble that paid homage to the goddess of love.

DUCT TAPE
white (heavy duty), 6 yd (5.5m)
gold chrome, 4 yd (3.7m)
silver chrome, 4 yd (3.7m)

ADDITIONAL MATERIALS
parchment paper, 11" × 18"
   (28cm × 45.5cm)
printout of template (see page 208),
   trimmed to outline of shape
4 neodymium magnets, ½" (13mm)
   diameter, ¹⁄₁₆" (1.5mm) thick

TOOLS
• scissors
• craft knife
• metal ruler
• white grease pencil
• black grease pencil

1 Place the parchment paper on the worktable in the portrait position and make a duct tape fabric (see page 10) using 11 strips of 12" (30.5cm) white duct tape for the back side and 7 strips of 19" (48.5cm) gold chrome duct tape for the front side. Trim the fabric to 11" × 18" (28cm × 45.5cm).

2 Place the fabric, gold side facing up, in a portrait position. //A Place the template on top of the fabric so the scalloped side is about ½" (13mm) from the top edge. Use the grease pencil to trace the shape of the clamshell onto the gold side of the fabric.//

A

Flip the template over so the scalloped edge is near the bottom of the gold fabric and trace its mirror image. Cut out the clamshell shapes from the fabric. These are the front and back of the bag. Set the clamshell shapes aside and discard the extra fabric.

3 Place the bottom half of the parchment paper over the clamshell template. Trace the outside clamshell shape as well as the inside curved lines onto the parchment paper.

//B Flip over the parchment paper and place the blank area over the clamshell template. Trace the outside clamshell shape and inside curved lines again for the mirror image.**//**

4 TO MAKE THE CLAMSHELL STICKERS, cover one side of the parchment paper lengthwise with 7 strips of 19" (48.5cm) silver chrome duct tape. As you place each strip, be sure to overlap the long edges of the previous one by approximately ¼" (6mm), creating a one-sided duct tape fabric.

5 Flip over the silver chrome fabric so that the parchment paper is facing up. You will be able to see the tracings from step 3. Cut out both outer clamshell shapes.

6 Match one of the stickers, leaving it on the parchment paper so the sticky side is not yet exposed, with one of the finished bag fabric pieces. Be sure the front of the silver chrome and the front of the gold chrome are facing up.

//C Flip over the sticker and cut out every other curved column of the clamshell plus the base. Remove the parchment paper from the back of the silver column stickers and place each one onto the bag fabric in its matching spot.**//**

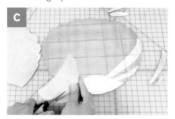

Discard the excess sticker. Repeat with the remaining silver chrome clamshell sticker and bag fabric piece.

7 TO MAKE A BAG SIDE, cut and place a 4½" (11.5cm) white duct tape strip on the worktable in a vertical position, sticky side facing up. Cut another 4½" (11.5cm) white duct tape strip and place it vertically on top of the first strip, sticky side facing down, so that it covers only half of the first strip. **//D** Cut a third 4½" (11.5cm) white duct tape strip and place it vertically on the opposite side of the second strip, sticky side facing down, covering the remaining exposed side of the first strip.**//**

The top 2 strips should each have approximately a 1" (2.5cm) section of the sticky side remaining exposed on the outer edges.

8 //E From the top corners of these connected strips, measure down 2½" (6.5cm) along the left and right edges and mark with a grease pencil.**//**

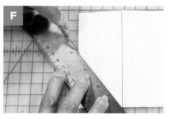

//F From these 2 points, draw diagonal lines to the middle of the bottom edge.**//**

//G Cut the tape along these diagonal lines into a point, removing the 2 bottom corners.**//**

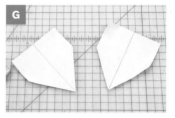

9 Repeat steps 7 and 8 to make the second bag side.

10 **TO FINISH THE BAG,** place one of the clamshell main bag pieces on the worktable with the white duct tape side facing up. Be sure the scalloped edge is at the top. **//H** Approximately 2" (5cm) from the bottom, lightly draw with a black grease pencil a rectangle 7" × 4½" (18cm × 11.5cm) on the fabric.**//**

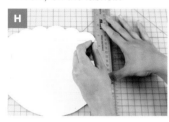

11 Because of the way they are constructed, the bag sides have natural creases for an accordion fold. **//I** Follow the natural creases created by the tape and fold them into M shapes by pulling back on the outer sticky edges.**//**

Hold one of the bag sides in the vertical position, pointed end at the bottom and sticky outer edge facing out.

//J Place the right sticky edge of the bag side on the right edge of the rectangle drawn on the fabric.**//**

Take the second bag side and hold it in the vertical position, pointed end at the bottom and sticky outer edge facing out. **//K** Place the left sticky edge of the bag side on the left edge of the rectangle drawn on the fabric.**//**

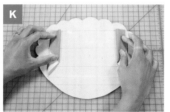

//L While holding down the bag sides in the folded position, place the remaining bag piece on top of the bottom bag piece, white duct tape side facing down.**//**

Be sure to line up the edges of the clamshell shape. The sticky edges of the bag sides should stick to the top bag piece.

12 **//M** The bottom of the bag pocket is unattached.**//** From inside the bag, place a 7" (18cm) strip of white duct tape horizontally between the front and back pieces to close the pocket. The bag now has an accordion-like opening, with the closed end at the base of the clamshell shape.

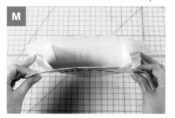

13 With 2 strips of 5" (12.5cm) white duct tape, attach the 4 neodymium magnets to the top opening of the bag (see page 14), 2 magnets per side.

HOBO & SHOULDER BAG

There are designer hobo bags that can fetch retail prices as high as $25,000—the cost of a brand-new car! So when you see one with a Louis Vuitton or Gucci logo, you may automatically think, "There goes a Fiat." Most hobo and shoulder bags aren't *that* extravagant, but they are still fancier than a flap or messenger bag. You can carry one proudly to a four-star restaurant. Personally, I've actually stuffed my trench coat into a shoulder bag and then slung it over the back of my chair at Del Posto in New York City. No one batted an eye.

The hobo and shoulder bags in this section convey that same allusion to grandeur, which is extraordinary considering that the cost of materials is about $15 per project. They require a little more time and patience than the clutches, but they are well worth it.

GRANNY SMITH

The combination of green and brown makes me think of my favorite apples: Granny Smiths. So I made a bag that pays homage to that sweet-and-sour fruit. This shoulder bag, however, is anything but granny-like. The pleats give it an updated prep school appeal, and I can picture it slung over a blazer. And in addition to biochemistry textbooks or a classic novel, you can probably fit an apple or two inside—a perfect gift from the teacher's pet.

DUCT TAPE
white (heavy duty), 17 yd (15.5m)
sour apple linen Platypus Designer Duct Tape, 11 yd (10m)
mahogany Platypus Designer Duct Tape, 5 yd (4.6m)

ADDITIONAL MATERIALS
parchment paper, 17½" × 11½" (44.5cm × 29cm)
parchment paper, 14" × 9½" (35.5cm × 24cm)
printout of template (see page 199), trimmed to outline shape
magnetic snap closure, ¾" (2cm) diameter

TOOLS
• scissors
• craft knife
• metal ruler
• black grease pencil
• flat-nose pliers

1 Place the larger piece of parchment paper on the worktable in the landscape position. Make the back side of a duct tape fabric (see page 10) using 7 strips of 18½" (47cm) white duct tape. After completing the back side, flip the working fabric over so the parchment paper is facing up. Trim the fabric to 17½" × 11½" (44.5cm × 29cm). Gently peel off the parchment paper, exposing the sticky side of the fabric. Set aside.

2 **TO MAKE THE PLEATS FOR THE FRONT SIDE OF THE FABRIC,** cut 10 strips of 12½" (32cm) sour apple linen duct tape. Place them with the sticky side facing up. Fold back one of the long edges approximately ⅛" (3mm) on each strip.

3 Place the working fabric in the landscape position on the worktable. You will now add the sour apple linen pleats to the sticky side of the fabric, perpendicular to the direction of the strips on the back side. Line up the first pleat with the outer left edge of the fabric and attach the pleat; the long folded edge of the pleat should be on the left. Add the next pleat so that it barely overlaps the first pleat, again with the folded edge on the left side. //NOTE: Platypus tape is thicker than other brands of duct tape. Folds in the duct tape will eventually unfold, so be sure the pleats are not overlapping any more than ¹⁄₁₆" (1.5mm).//

Repeat with 3 more pleats for a total of 5. //**A** Line up the first pleat with the outer right edge of the fabric so that the folded edge is on the right; repeat with the remaining 4 pleats. There should be a space in the center of the 5 pleats on the right and the 5 on the left.//

4 **TO MAKE THE CENTER PLEAT,** cut a 12½" (32cm) strip of mahogany duct tape and fold back both long edges approximately ⅛" (3mm). //**B** Place the pleat in the center of the fabric.// Trim the height of the fabric to 11½" (29cm).

5 Repeat steps 1–4 to make the second fabric.

6 **TO MAKE THE FRONT AND BACK OF THE BAG,** place the fabrics on the worktable in the landscape position, white pleated duct tape sides facing up. Place the template on the lower left corner of one fabric,

aligning the straight edges. Use the grease pencil to trace the outside shape onto the fabric. Flip the template over from left to right for its mirror image and align the straight edges on the right side. Trace the outside shape onto the fabric. //**C** Cut out the complete shape from the fabric. Repeat on the other fabric.// Discard any extra fabric.

7 To attach the 2 sides of the bag to each other, cut a 36" (91cm) strip of white duct tape. //**D** Starting from the top corner of one outer edge, carefully attach the white tape to the back side of one of the fabrics so that only half of each 36" (91cm) strip is on the fabric lengthwise; continue down along the curved bottom edge and up the side of one of the fabrics.//

8 Flip the fabric over so the pleated side is facing up. //**E** Align the second fabric

with the edges of the first fabric, pressing the sticky half of the strip of tape against the back side of the second fabric to attach it.//

9 Measure 3" (7.5cm) from the top of each side seam and mark these points with a grease pencil. Turn the bag upside down. //**F** At the 3" (7.5cm) mark on the seams, push and fold in the corner ½" (13mm).//

On the inside of the bag, place small strips of white duct tape behind each fold to secure them.

10 From the center of the bottom seam, measure and mark 3½" (9cm) to the left and to the right. //**G** Pinch and vertically fold the bag against the bottom seam at these two marks, folding inward approximately ½" (13mm).// Place small pieces of white duct tape inside the bag to secure the folds. Set the bag aside.

(continued on next page)

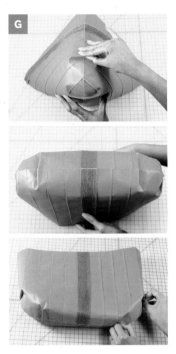

11 **TO MAKE THE FLAP OF THE BAG,** place the smaller piece of parchment paper on the worktable. Make the back side of a fabric using 8 strips of the 15" (38cm) white duct tape. After completing the back side, flip the working fabric over so the parchment paper is facing up. Trim the fabric to 14" wide × 9½" tall (35.5cm × 24cm). Gently peel off the parchment paper, exposing the sticky side of the fabric. Set aside.

12 **TO MAKE THE PLEATS FOR THE FRONT SIDE OF THE FLAP,** cut 8 strips of 13½" (34.5cm) sour apple linen duct tape and place them on the worktable with the sticky

sides facing up. Fold back one long edge approximately ⅛" (3mm) on each strip.

13 Place the working fabric in the landscape position on the worktable. Add the sour apple linen pleats on top of the fabric, perpendicular to the direction of the strips on the back side. Line up the first pleat with the outer left edge of the fabric and attach the pleat; the long folded edge of the pleat should be on the left. Add the next pleat so that it barely overlaps the first pleat, again with the folded edge on the left side. Repeat with 2 more pleats for a total of 4. Starting at the outer right edge of the fabric, line up the folded side of the first pleat with the outer right edge so that the folded edge is on the right. Repeat with the remaining 3 pleats. There should be a space in the center of the 4 pleats on the right and the 4 on the left.

14 **TO MAKE THE CENTER PLEAT,** cut a 10½" (26.5cm) strip of mahogany duct tape and fold both long edges back approximately ⅛" (3mm). Place it in the center of the fabric. Trim the height of the fabric to 9½" (24cm).

15 Place the flap on the worktable so the pleats are in the vertical position. From the left bottom corner measure and mark with a grease pencil

4½" (11.5cm) up along the left edge. From the center of the bottom edge, measure and mark with a grease pencil 3" (7.5cm) toward the left side. **//H** From these points, trim off the bottom left corner in a curved line, starting at the 4½" (11.5cm) mark and ending at the 3" (7.5cm) mark, rounding it. Take the cut corner piece and align the straight edges with the bottom right corner of the flap. Trace its curved line on the flap and remove it. Trim off the bottom right corner along the traced line. The rounded cut corners of the flap should be symmetrical.**//**

16 Place the main bag on the worktable so that the opening is at the bottom. Turn the flap over so that the white side faces up and align the top edge of the flap with the edge of the bag opening. **//I** Attach the flap to the bag with a 14" (35.5cm) strip of white duct tape.**//**

17 **TO MAKE THE STRAP:** You will make the strap in 3 pieces. //J Make the first 2 pieces of the strap by cutting two 20" (51cm) strips of mahogany duct tape. Fold back both long edges of each strip approximately ⅛" (3mm); set aside.// You will finish making the strap in step 19.

18 At each side seam, measure 6" (15cm) down from the top edge and mark these points with a grease pencil. //K Center and cut a 1½" (3.8cm) horizontal slit across each side seam at this point.//

//L Insert approximately 1" (2.5cm) of both 20" (51cm) strap pieces into the slits.//

Inside the bag, fold up the ends of the straps and place small pieces of white duct tape over the folded strap ends to attach them to the bag.

19 **TO FINISH THE STRAP,** cut a 14" (35.5cm) piece of mahogany duct tape. Fold back both long edges approximately ⅛" (3mm). //M With the sticky side still facing up, mark the center of this piece with a grease pencil.//

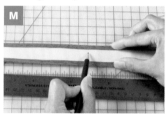

Cut 2 strips of 23" (58.5cm) white duct tape and trim each one down to 1⅛" (2.9cm) wide. //N Starting at the center mark on the 14" (35.5cm) mahogany strip, attach a 23" (58.5cm) strip of white duct tape to the left side of the mahogany strip; the rest of this strip will hang loose for now.// Repeat with the other 23" (58.5cm) strip of white duct tape.

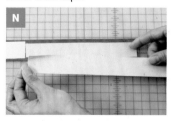

20 //O To complete the straps that are attached to the bag so that you have one continuous mahogany strap, adhere the loose end of one of the white duct tape strips about 9" (23cm) long to the sticky back side of the mahogany strap already attached to one side of the bag.//

Repeat on the other side. The white strips should be longer than the strap pieces and attach to the inside of the bag.

21 //P Wrap a 2" (5cm) strip of mahogany duct tape over each section on the strap where the pieces connect.//

22 Use 2 strips of 4" (10cm) white duct tape to center and attach the magnetic snap closure (see page 12) ½" (13mm) from the edge of the flap.

PEACOCK BAG

Aside from wristlets like the Summer Fling (page 18), this is one of the quickest and easiest bags to make. Yet the end result is no less sophisticated in appearance than one requiring more time and effort. You need to make only one medium-size fabric, and there is no template to trace. It also has an adjustable strap. I'm very proud of this design, which is why I used the motif of a very proud bird for the fabric. This is one of those bags that truly show off the attractive colors, prints, and patterns that duct tape has to offer.

DUCT TAPE
black (heavy duty), 8 yd (7.3m)
peacock, 6 yd (5.5m)
dark blue, 4 yd (3.7m)

ADDITIONAL MATERIALS
parchment paper, 17" × 15"
    (43cm × 38cm)
2 metal sliders, 1½" (3.8cm) wide

TOOLS
• scissors
• craft knife
• metal ruler
• white grease pencil

1 Place the parchment paper on the worktable in the landscape position and make a duct tape fabric (see page 10) using 10 strips of 18" (45.5cm) black duct tape for the back side and 9 strips of 17" (43cm) peacock duct tape for the front side. Trim the fabric to 16" × 17" (40.5cm × 43cm).

2 Place a 16½" (42cm) strip of dark blue duct tape on the worktable with the sticky side facing up. Fold back one long edge of the tape approximately ⅛" (3mm).

3 Place the fabric in the portrait position with the peacock side facing up. **// A** *Attach the folded dark blue duct tape strip, aligning its nonfolded long edge with the top edge of the peacock fabric.//* Place a second 16½" (42cm) strip of dark blue duct tape above the first dark blue strip on the fabric. The bottom long edge of the second strip should overlap the first strip by ¼" (6mm) and extend above the top edge of the fabric approximately 1" (2.5cm). Fold the dark blue tape strip over the top edge of the fabric and press it down on the black side.

4 With the black side facing up, place a 17" (43cm) black duct tape strip vertically on the right edge so that only half of the strip is on the fabric lengthwise. Fold back the tape strip so the sticky half is facing up. Refold the fabric in half vertically and line up the left edge with the right edge. Reposition and press down the folded tape strip to secure the side seam.

5 //B Refold the fabric so that the closed seam lies vertically in the center.//

Pull up the bottom edge of the fabric layer on top. Place an 8" (20.5cm) black duct tape strip horizontally on the bottom edge of the fabric layer underneath so that only half of the strip is on the fabric lengthwise. Fold back the tape strip so the unattached sticky half is facing up. Push the top fabric layer back down and line up the bottom edges of both the top and bottom layers. Reposition and press down the folded tape strip to secure the seam.

6 To flatten the bottom of the bag, starting at the bottom corners, measure 1½" (3.8cm) inward from each corner and mark these points with a grease pencil along the bottom edge. //C Pinch each corner into a triangle.//

Fold the point of the triangle down and inward along the bottom of the bag, making a perpendicular line at the 1½" (3.8cm) mark. //D Hold the corners in place with small pieces of black tape.//

//E Cover the bottom seam with a 4¾" (12cm) strip of peacock duct tape.//

7 TO MAKE A SHOULDER STRAP, cut a 48" (122cm) strip of black duct tape and a 48" (122cm) strip of dark blue duct tape. Stick them together. Cut the width down to 1½" (3.8cm).

8 From the top edge of the bag opening, measure 5" (12.5cm) down on both the right and left edges and mark these points with the grease pencil. Use the ruler to draw a horizontal line across the bag between these points. //F Hold the strap so the dark blue side is facing up. Place the top edge of the middle section of the strap below the 5" (12.5cm) line on the bag.//

//G Cover this part of the strap with a 7" (18cm) horizontal strip of peacock duct tape.// This is where the bag will fold horizontally to close the opening.

9 Loop a metal slider through one end of the shoulder strap, leaving a 2" (5cm) tail. //H Fold the tail over and secure it with a 1" (2.5cm) strip of dark blue duct tape.//

10 Measure 1" (2.5cm) down from the top edge of the bag opening and draw a 1¾" (4.5cm) horizontal line in the center with the grease pencil. //I Using the line as a guide, cut through both the front and back of the bag.//

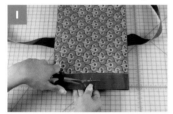

11 Fold the top portion of the bag down over the shoulder strap at the 5" (12.5cm) mark. //J Using a grease pencil, draw a line through the opening you made in step 10 on the surface underneath it.//

Unfold the bag and cut a 1¾" (4.5cm) slit along the drawn line through the top layer of the bag only. Cut a second 1¾" (4.5cm) horizontal slit 2" (5cm) directly below the first line.

12 **TO MAKE THE CLOSURE STRAP,** cut a 24" (61cm) strip of black duct tape and a 24" (61cm) strip of dark blue duct tape. Stick them together. Cut the width down to 1½" (3.8cm).

13 Hold the closure strap in the vertical position with the black duct tape side facing up. //K Push the top end of the closure strap through the bottom slit and into the bag. Pull the top end of the closure strap out through the top slit.//

Pull the closure strap up until there is a 2½" (6.5cm) tail at the end of the closure strap that starts at the bottom slit.

14 Loop a metal slider through the bottom end of the strap, leaving a 1" (2.5cm) tail. //L Fold the tail over the middle bar of the slider and secure it with a 1" (2.5cm) strip of dark blue duct tape.//

15 To close the bag, fold the top portion downward over the shoulder strap at the 5" (12.5cm) mark and pull the top edge of the bag down. //M Push the top edge of the closure strap through the slits near the top edge of the bag and fasten it through the slider bar.//

NOT FOR
THE LINKS

This bag is named after some inventive golf fashion. Professional golfers are not really known for their flamboyant sartorial choices, but have you ever seen photos of the Swedish golfer Jesper Parnevik? He has been known to wear tartan berets with pom-poms and knickers. I thought it would be fun to use plaid touches on a silver chrome shoulder bag. It's fun and a bit preppy in that nonsensical way that Jesper Parnevik dresses. And while this bag is certainly not for the links, you can use it to throw in those locker-room essentials for your post-game cooldown.

DUCT TAPE
white (heavy duty), 11 yd (10m)
silver chrome, 14 yd (12.8m)
pink plaid, 6 yd (5.5m)

ADDITIONAL MATERIALS
parchment paper, 14½" × 15"
    (37cm × 38cm)
printout of template (see page 198),
    trimmed to outline of shape
1 jeans button, ¾" (2cm) diameter

TOOLS
• scissors
• craft knife
• metal ruler
• graphite pencil
• white grease pencil
• hammer

1 For this project you will need 2 identical fabrics. Place the parchment paper on the worktable in the landscape position and make the first duct tape fabric (see page 10) using 9 strips of 16¼" (41cm) white duct tape for the back side and 9 strips of 15½" (39.5cm) silver chrome duct tape for the front side. Trim the fabric to 14½" × 15¼" (37cm × 38.5cm). Repeat to make the second fabric. Set

aside the parchment paper for step 4.

2 **TO MAKE THE FRONT AND BACK OF THE BAG,** //A place the template on the silver side of one fabric and use the grease pencil to trace the outside shape onto it. //Repeat with the second fabric. Cut out the shapes from the fabric and set aside. Discard any extra fabric.

A

3 **TO MAKE THE ALTERNATING PINK PLAID AND SILVER CHROME PLEATS** for the front of the bag, cut 8 strips of 15½" (39.5cm) silver

chrome duct tape and 8 strips of 15½" (39.5cm) pink plaid duct tape. Flip the strips over so the sticky sides are facing up. Fold back one of the long edges approximately ⅛" (3mm) on each strip.

4 Use the graphite pencil and ruler to draw 2 horizontal lines 3½" (9cm) apart from each other on the reserved parchment paper. Hold a pink plaid pleat lengthwise, sticky side facing down and folded edge at the top. Place it on the parchment paper, aligning the folded edge with the upper horizontal line. Hold a silver chrome pleat in the same manner and place it on top of the pink plaid pleat, leaving ¼" (6mm) of the pink plaid visible. Place a second pink plaid pleat on top of the silver chrome pleat, leaving ¼" (6mm) of the silver chrome visible. Repeat with another silver chrome pleat. You should now have 4 staggered and alternating pleats at the upper horizontal line on the parchment paper.

5 Hold a pink plaid pleat lengthwise, sticky side facing down and folded edge at the bottom. Place it on the parchment paper, aligning the folded edge with the bottom horizontal line. Hold a silver chrome pleat in the same manner and place it on top of

the pink plaid pleat, leaving ¼" (6mm) of the pink plaid visible. Place a second pink plaid pleat on top of the silver chrome pleat, leaving ¼" (6mm) of the silver chrome visible. Repeat with another silver chrome pleat. You should now have 4 staggered and alternating pleats at the bottom horizontal line on the parchment paper.

6 **TO MAKE THE DECORATIVE BAND** that goes between the 2 sets of pleats, cut a 15½" (39.5cm) strip of pink plaid duct tape and fold back approximately ⅛" (3mm) on both long edges of the tape. //B Center and place this band lengthwise in the space between the 2 sets of pleats.//

7 Place one of the bag fabrics on the worktable, silver side facing up and the wider end at the bottom. From the bottom corners of the fabric, measure up 5" (12.5cm) on the left and right edges and mark these points with a grease pencil. Lightly draw a horizontal line connecting the 2 marks. Remove the parchment paper from the back of the decorative band from step 6.

//C Align the bottom edge of the band with the horizontal line you drew on the bag and place the band on the fabric.// Trim the outer edges of the band to match the edges of the fabric.

8 **TO MAKE THE PLEATS AND DECORATIVE BAND** for the back of the bag, repeat steps 4–7 using the same parchment paper.

9 Place the fabrics on the worktable, the white duct tape side facing up, one above the other so they are mirror images with a seam in the middle. Connect the 2 fabrics by placing a 14½" (37cm) strip of white duct tape over the seam. Starting from the bottom corners of the top fabric only, place a 14½" (37cm) strip of white duct tape vertically on each of the left- and right-hand edges so that only half of the strip is on the fabric lengthwise. Fold back the tape strips lengthwise so the sticky half is facing up. Pull the bottom fabric up over the top fabric, folding at the middle seam. Line up the left and right edges of the 2 fabrics and press down the folded tape strips to secure the sides.

10 To flatten the bottom of the bag, measure 2" (5cm) inward along the bottom edge from both corners and mark these points with a grease pencil. //D Pinch each corner into a triangle. Fold the point of the triangles down and inward along the bottom of the bag, making a perpendicular line at the 2" (5cm) mark.// Hold the corners in place with small pieces of silver chrome tape.

11 To secure the side seams, cut a 40" (101.5cm) strip of pink plaid duct tape. //E Starting at the top of one of the side seams, use this strip to cover the seam down one side, across the bottom, and up the other side.// Trim any excess tape at the ends.

12 TO MAKE THE STRAPS, cut 2 strips of 22" (56cm) pink plaid duct tape and fold each of them lengthwise into thirds.

13 You will notice that there are 2 sets of extensions at the top of the bag, one set per bag side. //F Place the ends of a strap on top of a set of extensions so they overlap by approximately ½" (13mm). Starting on the back side of each extension, attach a 1" (2.5cm) strip of silver chrome duct tape and wrap it around the extension and strap.// Repeat on the remaining strap and set of extensions.

14 TO MAKE THE TONGUE SECTION OF THE CLOSURE, cut one 7" (18cm) strip of white duct tape and one 7" (18cm) strip of silver chrome duct tape. Stick them together. To make the pink plaid detail on the tongue, cut a 7" (18cm) strip of pink plaid duct tape and flip it over so the sticky side is facing up. Fold back both long edges approximately ⅛" (3mm). Center this strip lengthwise on the silver chrome side of the tongue and stick them together.

15 On one side of the bag, cut a 2" (5cm) horizontal slit in the center approximately 1½" (3.8cm) below the top

edge. //G Insert one end of the tongue about 1" (2.5cm) deep.//

On the inside of the bag, place a 3" (7.5cm) strip of white duct tape lengthwise over the inserted end of the tongue to secure it to the inside of the bag.

16 //H On the front side of the unattached end of the tongue, cut a ½" (13mm) horizontal slit approximately 1" (2.5cm) from the edge, then carefully cut the slit into an elongated spheroid (football shape).//

Close the top of the bag and pull the tongue down until the top of the bag is comfortably closed. Push a grease pencil through the hole and mark the front of the bag. Release the tongue and attach a jeans button at the mark (see page 13).

AMAGANSETT

This bag was actually inspired by the duct tape pattern itself: white linen. It's a very subtle print and one that calls out to be made into a bag. White linen duct tape actually becomes white linen "fabric," which makes me think of well-heeled people who live on the beach, drive vintage convertibles, and wear crisp shirts that show off their tan lines.

DUCT TAPE
black (heavy duty), 12 yd (10.9m)
white linen, 9 yd (8.2m)
mahogany Platypus Designer Duct Tape,
    5 yd (4.6m)

ADDITIONAL MATERIALS
parchment paper, 15½" × 12"
    (39.5cm × 30.5cm)
printout of template (see page 198),
    trimmed to outline of shape
jeans button, ¾" (2cm) diameter

TOOLS
• scissors
• craft knife
• metal ruler
• black grease pencil
• hammer

1 For this project you will need 2 identical fabrics. Place the parchment paper on the worktable in the portrait position and make the first duct tape fabric (see page 10) using 10 strips of 13" (33cm) black duct tape for the back side and 8 strips of 16½" (42cm) white linen duct tape for the front side. Trim the fabric to 15½" × 12" (39.5cm × 30.5cm). Repeat to make a second fabric.

2 **TO MAKE THE FRONT AND BACK OF THE BAG,** place the fabrics on the worktable in the landscape position, white linen side facing up. Place the template on the upper left corner of one fabric. Use the grease pencil to trace the outside shape onto the fabric. Flip the template over for its mirror image. Trace the outside shape onto the right corner of the fabric.

//A Cut out the complete shape from the fabric.**//** Repeat with the other fabric. Discard any extra fabric.

3 Place the fabrics on the worktable, black duct tape side facing up, with one above the other so they are mirror images with a seam in the middle. Connect the two fabrics by placing a 15½" (39.5cm) strip of black duct tape over the seam. //B Starting from the bottom corners of the top fabric only, place an 11" (28cm) strip of black duct tape vertically on each of the left and right edges so that only half of each strip is on the fabric lengthwise. Fold back the tape strips so the sticky half is facing up.//

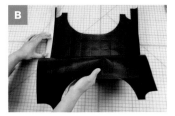

//C Pull the bottom fabric up over the top fabric, folding at the middle seam.//

Line up the left and right edges of the two fabrics, and press down the folded tape strips to secure the sides.

4 To flatten the bottom of the bag, measure 2" (5cm) inward along the bottom edge from both bottom corners and mark these points with a grease pencil. Pinch each corner into a triangle. //D Fold the point of each triangle down and inward along the bottom of the bag, making a perpendicular line at the 2" (5cm) mark. Hold each corner in place with a small piece of black tape.//

//E Cover the bottom of the bag with 2 strips of 10½" (26.5cm) linen duct tape, one on top of the other.//

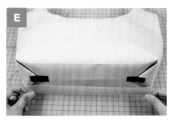

5 Place the template on the worktable and cover it with the parchment paper. To make the stickers for the mahogany borders of the bag, first move the template to the top left edge of the parchment paper and trace the template. Then flip over the parchment paper so the mirror image of the tracing

can be seen. Move the template to the top left edge of the parchment paper again, lining up the left edge of the tracing with the right edge of the template. Trace the template to complete the border tracing.

6 There should be room on the bottom half of the parchment paper to repeat step 5. //F You now have 2 complete border tracings on the parchment paper.//

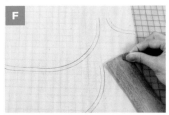

7 Cover the tracings with 8 strips of 10" (25.5cm) mahogany duct tape. As you place each strip, be sure to overlap the long edges of the previous one by approximately ¼" (6mm), creating a one-sided duct tape fabric. Flip over the parchment paper so you can see the tracings. //G Cut out the borders with scissors.//

8 **TO MAKE THE STRAP,** cut a 25" (63.5cm) strip of black duct tape and a 25" (63.5cm) strip of mahogany duct tape; stick them together. Cut the width down to 1" (2.5cm). Repeat to make the second strap.

9 //H Peel off the parchment paper and place the stickers on the top edges of the bag.//

You will notice that there are 2 sets of extensions at the top of the bag, one set of extensions per each bag side. Place the ends of one strap next to the tops of a set of extensions so they meet.
//I On the back side of each extension and strap end, attach a 1" (2.5cm) strip of black duct tape. Stick a 1" (2.5cm) strip of mahogany duct tape on the front side of each extension and strap end. Wrap it around the extension and strap.//

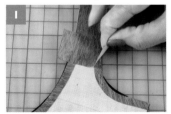

Trim the tape to match the curved shape of the bag extensions. Repeat on the sides.

10 **TO MAKE THE TONGUE OF THE CLOSURE,** create a double-sided strip by sticking together a 6" (15cm) strip of black duct tape and a 6" (15cm) strip of mahogany duct tape. Cut off the corners on one end of the tongue in a curved line, rounding them.

11 On one side of the bag, cut a 2" (5cm) horizontal slit in the center approximately 1½" (3.8cm) below the top edge. //J Insert the straight end of the tongue 1" (2.5cm) deep.//

On the inside of the bag, place a 4" (10cm) strip of black duct tape lengthwise over the inserted portion of the tongue to secure it to the inside of the bag.

12 On the front side of the unattached end of the tongue, cut a ½" (13mm) horizontal slit approximately 1" (2.5cm) from the edge, then carefully cut the slit into an elongated spheroid (football shape). Close the top of the bag and pull the tongue down until the top of the bag is comfortably closed. //K Push a grease pencil through the hole and mark the front of the bag.// Release the tongue and attach a jeans button at the mark (see page 13).

SERENA

The name Serena means "peaceful one." But do you want to know what I think of when I hear that name? I imagine a fashionable, sporty type emulating the current Serenas in our pop culture. She is a worldly peripatetic, a lover of art and a good pair of shoes. Random and yet full of purpose, Serena is a person who needs to feel life happening around her. This bag suits the Serena in all of us. It's got a classic duotone design that can go from the gym to a business luncheon, do some heavy lifting at an outdoor market, or serve as the vessel for a romantic picnic in the park.

DUCT TAPE
white (heavy duty), 15 yd (13.7m)
white (regular), 9 yd (8.2m)
Brazilian rosewood, 7 yd (6.4m)
gold chrome, 1yd (0.9m)

ADDITIONAL MATERIALS
parchment paper, 20" × 12½"
   (51cm × 32cm)
parchment paper, 16½" × 4"
   (42cm × 10cm)

TOOLS
• scissors
• craft knife
• metal ruler
• white grease pencil

1 For this project you will need 2 fabrics that you will cut in half for the main bag. Place the large parchment paper on the worktable in the landscape position and make a duct tape fabric (see page 10) using 8 strips of 21" (53.5cm) white heavy-duty tape for the back side and 12 strips of 13½" (34.5cm) white regular duct tape for the front side. Trim the fabric to 20" x 12½" (51cm × 32cm). Cut it in half vertically to make two 10" × 12½" (25.5cm × 32cm) fabrics. This is the first set of fabrics. Set aside.

2 Repeat step 1, but use 8 strips of 21" (53.5cm) white heavy-duty duct tape for the back side and 12 strips of 13½" (34.5cm) Brazilian rosewood duct tape for the front side. Cut it in half vertically to make two 10" × 12½" (25.5cm × 32cm) fabrics. This is the second set of fabrics.

3 **TO MAKE ONE SIDE OF THE BAG,** use one of the all-white fabrics and one of the Brazilian rosewood fabrics. Flip them both over so the white heavy-duty duct tape side is facing up, and line them up vertically with the 12½" (32cm) edges touching. Connect the 2 pieces with a strip of 13" (33cm) white heavy-duty duct tape, placing it over the adjacent edges and creating one 20" × 12½" (51cm × 32cm) fabric.

4 //**A** Repeat step 3 on the remaining white and Brazilian rosewood fabrics to make the other side of the bag.//

5 Place one of the fabrics on the worktable with the white regular duct tape side on the left and the Brazilian rosewood duct tape side on the right. Flip the fabric from top to bottom so the white heavy-duty duct tape side is facing up, with the white side still on the left and the Brazilian rosewood on the right on the sides that are facing down. Hold the second fabric so the Brazilian rosewood side is on the left and the white side is on the right. Place the second fabric directly on top of the first fabric with the white heavy-duty sides together. Lift up the top fabric and place a 13" (33cm) strip of heavy-duty white duct tape vertically on each of the left- and right-hand edges, starting at the bottom corners of the fabric so that only half of each strip is on the fabric underneath. //**B** Fold back the tape strips so the sticky half is facing up. Re-cover the bottom fabric with the top fabric, lining up the left and right edges, and

press down the folded tape strips to secure the sides.// The bottom seam will remain open for now. Set aside.

6 **TO MAKE THE BOTTOM OF THE BAG,** place the small parchment paper on your worktable. Make a fabric using 3 strips of 17½" (44.5cm) white heavy-duty duct tape for the back side and 5 strips of 5" (12.5cm) Brazilian rosewood duct tape next to 5 strips of 5" (12.5cm) white regular duct tape for the front side. Cut the fabric to 16½" × 4" (42cm × 10cm). //**C** Starting approximately ¼" (6mm) from each corner, round the four corners of this fabric.//

7 To secure the bottom to the main bag, cut a 40" (101.5cm) strip of white heavy-duty duct tape. //**D** Attach half of the strip lengthwise along the entire inside bottom edge of the main bag (in other words, you

will be sticking this strip of tape to the white heavy-duty tape back side of the fabrics), leaving the other half of the sticky side of the tape exposed beyond the edge of the bag.//

8 //**E** Attach the bottom of the bag by aligning its edges with the edge of the main body and pressing the exposed tape strip against the all-white back side of the bottom.//

//**F** You will need to press the tape strip against the back side of the bag bottom in order to get a tight seam.//

9 **TO MAKE THE HORIZONTAL STRIPE DETAILS AT THE TOP OF THE BAG,** measure down 1" (2.5cm) from the top corners along the left and right edges and mark these points with a grease pencil. Lightly draw a horizontal line connecting the 2 marks across each bag side. Cut 2 strips of 20" (51cm) white regular duct tape. **//G** Starting at the left or right side seam, place each strip horizontally at the top of a bag side, aligning the bottom long edge of the strip with the grease-pencil line on the bag. Fold the strips over the top edge of the bag.**//**

10 Cut a 20" (51cm) strip of Brazilian rosewood tape lengthwise into 2 strips that measure ¼" (6mm) wide. **//H** On each side of the bag, place one of the strips horizontally ½" (13mm) below the top edge.**//**

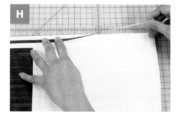

11 **TO MAKE THE STRAPS,** cut 2 strips of 26" (66cm) white regular duct tape in half lengthwise. **//I** Fold each strip lengthwise into thirds.**//**

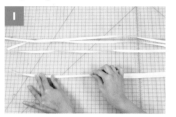

12 Place one pair of straps on top of each other. Be sure that they match up at each end. **//J** Measure 5" (12.5cm) from one end and wrap a ½" (13mm) strip of gold chrome tape around both pieces, connecting them. Measure 5" (12.5cm) from the other end and wrap a second ½" (13mm) strip of gold chrome duct tape around both pieces. Wrap each individual strap end with ½" (13mm) strip of gold chrome duct tape.**//**

13 Repeat step 12 for the remaining pair of straps.

14 Measure 3½" (9cm) to the right of the bag's vertical center (where the white fabric meets the Brazilian rosewood) at the top edge. Mark this point with the grease pencil. **//K** Using the grease pencil and a ruler, lightly draw a vertical line from this point downward approximately 2" (5cm).**//**

//L Measuring from the top edge along this marked line, cut two ½" (13mm) horizontal slits ¼" (6mm) and 1" (2.5cm) from the top of the bag.**//** Be sure the slits are directly below each other.

15 **//M** To attach the straps, starting from the front of the bag, weave one strap end of the gold-wrapped pair of straps through the top slit and back out the bottom slit.**//**

//N Pull down the strap end so that it hangs 3½" (9cm) from the top edge of the bag.**//**

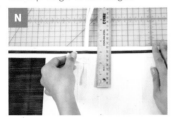

Place a small piece of white heavy-duty tape over the part of the strap that sits on the back side of the bag.

16 Repeat steps 14 and 15 to attach the strap to the left side of the bag's front.

17 Flip the bag over and repeat steps 14–16 to attach the strap on the other side of the bag. Wrap ½" (13mm) of gold duct tape strips around the ends of all the straps.

18 **TO MAKE THE SIDE STRAPS,** cut a 6" (15cm) strip of white regular duct tape in half lengthwise. Fold each strip lengthwise into thirds. Set aside.

19 Starting from the left top corner of the bag, measure and mark vertically down 1½" (3.8cm) along the side seam. From this point and moving horizontally to the left side, measure and mark 1½" (3.8cm) and 1¾" (4.5cm). Repeat on the right side of the side seam. **//O** Cut ½" (13mm) vertical slits at each of these points. Starting from the right top corner of the bag, repeat step. There should be a total of 8 slits: 4 on each side seam.**//**

20 Place the bag on the worktable so it is standing up and one of the side seams is facing toward you. Hold one end of a side strap. Starting from the outside, push the strap end through the farthest left slit. Moving toward the right, weave the strap end through the rest of the slits. **//P** Pull both strap ends until the space between the farthest left and farthest right slits measures 2" (5cm).**//**

Tuck the strap ends into the farthest left and farthest right slits. **//Q** Wrap a ½" (13mm) strip of gold chrome duct tape vertically around the middle of the side strap to hold it in place.**//**

21 **//R** Turn the bag so the other side seam faces you. Repeat step 20 with the remaining side strap.**//**

SOBE

In the section of Miami, Florida, known as South Beach, colors drench the atmosphere. Whether you are window-shopping along Collins Avenue or skating the length of the esplanade, everything and everyone are lit up from the inside out. If Neptune were to rise from the ocean here, carrying this flamingo-pink seashell bag, no one would look twice.

DUCT TAPE
white (heavy duty), 13 yd (11.8m)
hot pink, 11 yd (10m)
white (regular), 8 yd (7.3m)

ADDITIONAL MATERIALS
2 pieces of parchment paper, 14" × 11"
(35.5cm × 28cm)
printout of fish-scale template (see page 202),
trimmed to outline of shape
printout of bag template (see page 202),
trimmed to outline of shape
magnetic snap, ¾" (2cm) diameter

TOOLS
• scissors
• craft knife
• metal ruler
• graphite pencil
• white grease pencil

1 //**A** You will need 3 fabrics for this project.// Place one of the parchment paper pieces on the worktable and make the first duct tape fabric (see page 10), using 4 strips of 15" (38cm) white heavy-duty duct tape for the back side and 8 strips of 12" (30.5cm) hot pink duct tape for the front side. Trim the fabric to 14" × 11" (35.5cm × 28cm). Repeat this step twice. Set aside the 3 fabrics and the parchment paper, which will be reused for stickers in step 2.

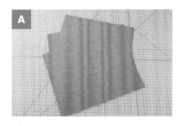

2 **TO MAKE THE FISH-SCALE STICKERS,** place one of the parchment papers over the fish-scale template. Using a graphite pencil, trace the entire sheet of fish scales onto the parchment paper. //**B** Completely fill the paper with fish scales, even if

it's a partial tracing. Repeat with the second parchment paper.//

3 Cut 14 strips of 15" (38cm) white regular duct tape. Cover one side of each of the parchment papers lengthwise with 7 of the strips. As you place each strip, be sure to overlap

67

XANADU

Diagonal stripes in purple, magenta, and pastel pink make me wax nostalgic for the 1980s. When I was a kid, I loved *Xanadu,* starring Olivia Newton-John and Gene Kelly. The plot was threadbare—something about a man inspired by a muse (Ms. Newton-John, of course) to open a disco roller rink. But I loved the songs and mostly the fashion. My Xanadu bag reminds me of the shiny shorts that some of us bravely wore to our Friday night skate parties.

DUCT TAPE
black (heavy duty), 15 yd (13.7m)
purple, 8 yd (7.3m)
magenta, 5 yd (4.6m)
pastel pink, 5 yd (4.6m)

ADDITIONAL MATERIALS
parchment paper, 18" × 15"
    (45.5cm × 38cm)
printout of bag template (see page 200),
    trimmed to outline of shape
4 O-rings, 1½" (3.8cm) diameter

TOOLS
• scissors
• craft knife
• metal ruler
• white grease pencil

1 You will need 2 fabrics to make this bag. Place the parchment paper on the worktable in the portrait position and make the first duct tape fabric (see page 10) using 11 strips of 16" (40.5cm) black duct tape for the back side. Flip the working fabric over so the parchment paper is facing up. Gently peel off the parchment paper, exposing the sticky side of the fabric. Place the fabric in the landscape position.

2 **TO MAKE THE FRONT SIDE OF ONE FABRIC,** cut 3 strips of 24" (61cm) purple duct tape, 3 strips of 24" (61cm) magenta duct tape, and 3 strips of 24" (61cm) pastel pink duct tape. Cut all 9 strips in half lengthwise. **//A** Starting at the top right corner of the parchment paper, place the strips on top of the fabric at a diagonal, working your way down toward the bottom left corner and overlapping the long edges of the strips by approximately ¹⁄₁₆" (1.5mm),

connecting them into one large piece.**//** Alternate the colors so they do not repeat. Trim the strips along the perimeter as you place them down. Discard any leftover strips. Trim the fabric to 15" high × 18" wide (38cm × 45.5cm).

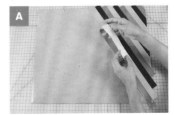

SATCHEL

For the most part, satchels are work-related bags. Meant to securely carry your important documents, they are usually rectangular in shape with a single handle or a pair of handles. The best-known example is a briefcase, which is what my college boyfriend gave me when I graduated. It was a soft, brown leather beauty that smelled as serious as I felt whenever I carried it. He expected me to be a lawyer or a banker, which is funny because I would sooner carry around craft supplies than an affidavit or a contract.

A satchel can nestle nicely in the crook of a secure elbow or be grasped with a confident hand. It still means business, but what type of business is entirely up to you.

MARY POPPINS

In the movie, Mary Poppins's satchel was a colorful carpetbag that could produce table lamps and coatracks. No furniture will pop out of this one, but the shape is certainly influenced by the original. Also, the single daisy on the front is a touch of Ms. Poppins herself, who sported a black brimmed hat with that practically perfect blossom.

DUCT TAPE
white (heavy duty), 11 yd (10m)
white (regular), 10 yd (9.1m)
black (heavy duty), 9 yd (8.2m)
floral, 2 yd (1.8m)

ADDITIONAL MATERIALS
parchment paper, 16" × 14"
    (40.5cm × 35.5cm)
printout of petal template (see page 198),
    trimmed to outline of shape
magnetic snap closure, ¾" (2cm) diameter

TOOLS
• scissors
• craft knife
• metal ruler
• black grease pencil
• circles inking template
• flat-nose pliers

1 For this project you will need 2 fabrics. Place the parchment paper on the worktable in the portrait position and make the first duct tape fabric (see page 10). Use 10 strips of 15" (38cm) white heavy-duty duct tape for the back side and 9 strips of 17" (43cm) white regular duct tape for the front side. Trim the fabric to 16" × 14" (40.5cm × 35.5cm). Repeat this step for the second fabric. Position the fabrics on the worktable in the landscape position, white regular duct tape side facing up.

2 **TO MAKE THE THIN BLACK HORIZONTAL STRIPE,** cut a 17" (43cm) strip of black duct tape and cut out 2 strips from it that are each ½" (13mm) wide. Discard the extra tape. From the top corners of one fabric, measure 5" (12.5cm) down along the left and right edges and mark with a grease pencil.

Draw a horizontal line across the fabric connecting the two points. Place one of the thin black strips lengthwise across the marked fabric, aligning the top long edge of the strip with the drawn line. Trim any part of this strip that extends past the outer edges of the fabric. Repeat this step with the remaining ½" (13mm) strip of black duct tape and the second fabric.

3 **TO CREATE THE VERTICAL FOLDS** in the bag, place one of the fabrics on the worktable in the landscape position with the white regular duct tape side facing up. Starting from the bottom left corner, measure 5" (12.5cm) inward along the bottom edge and mark it with the grease pencil. Starting from the bottom right corner, measure 5" (12.5cm) inward along the bottom edge and mark it with the grease pencil. **//A** At each mark, make a 1" (2.5cm) vertical fold at the bottom edge. The folds should face away from the center. Secure each fold on the back side of the fabric with a small piece of white heavy-duty duct tape.**//** Repeat this step on the other fabric.

4 **TO MAKE THE BAG'S MAIN POCKET,** place the fabrics on the worktable in the landscape position with the white heavy-duty duct tape side facing up. Place one fabric above the other so they are mirror images; the folded bottom edges of each fabric should meet and create a seam in the middle. **//B** Connect the 2 fabrics with a 16" (40.5cm) strip of white heavy-duty duct tape over the seam.**//**

5 **//C** Starting from the top corners of the connected fabric, place a 14" (35.5cm) strip of white heavy-duty duct tape vertically on the right and left edges. Be sure that only half of each strip is on the fabric lengthwise. Fold back the tape strip on the left edge so the sticky half is facing up.**//**

//D Pull up the bottom left edge of the fabric so that it aligns with the top left edge of the fabric, folding at the middle seam. Press down the folded tape strip to secure the sides.**//**

Repeat with a white tape strip on the right edge.

6 **TO MAKE THE BLACK BORDER AT THE TOP** of the bag, cut a 16" (40.5cm) strip

of black duct tape and hold it horizontally. **//E** On the front of the bag, place the long bottom edge of the strip 1" (2.5cm) below the top edge. Fold the rest of the strip over to the back side.**//** Turn the bag over and repeat this step with another strip of black duct tape.

7 To flatten the bottom of the bag, measure 2" (5cm) inward from the bottom corners along the bottom edge and mark with a grease pencil. **//F** Pinch each corner into a triangle. Fold the point of the triangle down and inward along the bottom of the bag, making a perpendicular line at the 2" (5cm) mark.**//**

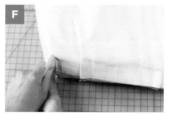

Secure the corners with pieces of white heavy-duty duct tape.

(continued on next page)

the left edge of the fabric's back side, but be sure to leave a hairline space between them. **//B** Carefully place the white strip down. Cut another 24" (61cm) strip of white duct tape and repeat this step on the right.**//**

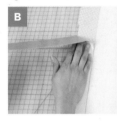

4 Trim the bottom of the entire fabric, including the sides, to match the bottom edge of the fabric's back side. Trim the width of each side to 1½" (3.8cm). Then horizontally trim the top of the fabric so the front side matches the height of the back side at 27½" (70cm). From each top corner, measure 4½" (11.5cm) down the left and right edges and mark these points with a grease pencil. Draw a horizontal line between these two points. **//C** Trim off the tops of the side pieces only along this line, leaving the upper portion of the main fabric intact.**//**

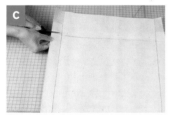

This upper portion, which now measures 14" × 4½" (35.5cm × 11.5cm), is the bag flap.

5 **TO MAKE THE MAIN POCKET OF THE BAG,** **//D** start from the bottom left corner of the fabric and place an 11½" (29cm) strip of white duct tape vertically on the left edge.**//**

Be sure only half of the strip is on the fabric lengthwise. Fold back the tape strip on the left edge so the sticky half is facing up. **//E** Pull up the bottom edge of the fabric and fold the fabric horizontally at 11½" (29cm). Line up the left edge and press the fabric down against the folded tape strip.**//** Repeat this step on the right edge.

6 To flatten the bottom of the bag, measure 1½" (3.8cm) inward from each corner along the bottom edge and mark with a grease pencil. Pinch each

corner into a triangle. **//F** Fold the point of the triangle down and inward along the bottom of the bag, making a perpendicular line at the 1½" (3.8cm) mark. Hold the corners in place with small pieces of white duct tape. Cover the bottom with 2 lengthwise strips of 12½" (32cm) houndstooth duct tape on top of each other, slightly overlapping.**//**

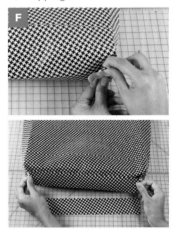

7 Position the bag on the worktable with the flap open and positioned at the bottom and the bag opening facing the worktable. From the top corners, measure 1" (2.5cm) up along the left and right edges and mark these points with a grease pencil. Using the ruler and grease pencil, draw a horizontal line connecting the 2 marks. Cut a 15½" (39.5cm) strip of black duct tape. **//G** Align one long bottom edge of the black tape strip, sticky side facing down,

with the horizontal line you drew on the flap; about half of the black strip will extend past the edge of the flap.//

Fold the excess at the top of the strip over the edge of the flap. Fold the sides of the strip over the outer edges of the flap.

8 Cut a 15½" (39.5cm) strip of red duct tape in half lengthwise. Place one of the half strips on the worktable so the sticky side is facing up. Fold back both of the long edges approximately ⅛" (3mm). //H Turn the strip over so the sticky side is facing down and, holding it lengthwise, place the strip on the bag flap, 1" (2.5cm) above the top edge.//

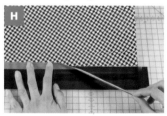

Fold the short sides of the strip over the outer edges of the flap. Discard the other half strip of red duct tape.

9 Flip the bag over so the bag opening is facing up and the flap is still open. //I Cut a 13½" (34.5cm) strip of white duct tape and place it, horizontally, approximately 1¹⁄₁₆" (2.7cm) below the top edge of the flap.//

This should cover the ends of both the black and red duct tape strips on the flap.

10 TO MAKE THE STRAPS, cut 2 strips of 37" (94cm) black duct tape and fold them both in half lengthwise.

11 Close the flap of the bag. //J Measure 1" (2.5cm) down below the closed flap on the right and left edges of the bag and mark these points with a grease pencil.// Lightly draw a horizontal line between them.

12 //K Starting 2" (5cm) from each outer edge, cut a 1¼" (3cm) horizontal slit along the line drawn in step 11. Insert 3" (7.5cm) of each end into the slits.//

To create a more natural curve for the handle, slightly angle the straps in toward the center of the bag. Cover the ends of the strap with 4½" (11.5cm) strips of white duct tape on the inside of the bag.

13 Flip the bag over. Be sure to keep the flap of the bag closed. Starting from the top corners, measure 5½" (14cm) down on the right and left edges of the back and mark these points with a grease pencil. Lightly draw a horizontal line between them. Repeat step 12 to attach the remaining strap to the back of the bag.

(continued on next page)

14 Use 2 strips of 4" (10cm) white duct tape to center and attach the magnetic snap closure (see page 12) ½" (13mm) from the edge of the flap.

15 **TO MAKE THE FLOWER ORNAMENT,** cut 2 strips of 15" (38cm) red duct tape and stick them directly on top of each other, creating a double-sided strip. **//M** Alternating the position of the flower petal template, trace it 12 times on the strip. Cut out the petals.**//**

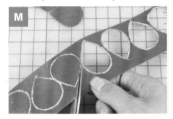

16 Using the circles inking template, draw a 1¾" (4.5cm) circle on a piece of black duct tape and cut out the circle. Place it on the worktable with the sticky side facing up. **//N** With the pointed ends of the petals facing the center of the circle, place the lower third of 4 petals onto the circle at the 3, 6, 9, and 12 o'clock positions.**//**

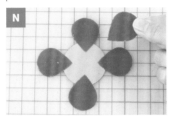

Place 4 more petals halfway onto the edge of the circle in between the previously placed petals. **//O** Place the remaining 4 petals inside the circle at the 3, 6, 9, and 12 o'clock positions, the pointed ends touching at the center. Cut a ½" (13mm) circle from a piece of red duct tape and place it in the center of the flower, covering the pointed ends of the petals.**//**

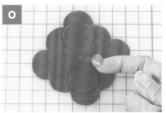

17 Cut 3 strips of ½" (13mm) black duct tape. With the sticky side facing out, attach the edges of the strips to each other to make a loop. **//P** Place the loop on the back of the flower and attach it to the center edge of the bag flap.**//**

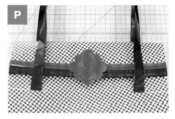

OAK PARK

Faux rosewood and tartan is a harmonious pairing, finding its inspiration in the windows of a Frank Lloyd Wright home. There is a formality to it, with checks and stripes dividing the rectangular plane of the bag. But the bright teal and white illuminate each square. Oak Park is serious retro fun, like a *Brady Bunch* episode; I can almost see Carol carrying it to a school meeting, wearing a color-block mini and big-buckle shoes.

DUCT TAPE
tan, 6 yd (5.5m)
teal, 8 yd (7.3m)
white (heavy duty), 13 yd (11.8m)
white linen, 1 yd (0.9m)
Brazilian rosewood, 8 yd (7.3m)

ADDITIONAL MATERIALS
parchment paper, 22" × 15"
(56cm × 38cm)
parchment paper, 7" × 8½"
(18cm × 21.5cm)

TOOLS
• scissors
• craft knife
• metal ruler
• black grease pencil

1 Place the 22" × 15" (56cm × 38cm) piece of parchment paper on the worktable in the landscape position and make the first duct tape fabric (see page 10). You will work on the front of the fabric first, which is woven. Cover the parchment paper horizontally with 8 strips of 24" (61cm) tan duct tape, leaving a hairline space between each strip.

2 Starting with the top strip, pull back every other strip of the tan duct tape past the left edge of the parchment paper. Be sure the strips stick to the worktable just beyond the left edge of the parchment paper. //**A** Place a 16½" (42cm) strip of teal duct tape vertically on top of the remaining tan duct tape strips, lining up the left long edge of the teal strip with the left edge

of the parchment paper, and extending approximately ½"–¾" (13mm–2cm) past the top and bottom edges of the parchment paper.//

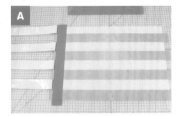

Replace the tan duct tape strips that were pulled back. This is the first column. //**B** Pull back the remaining tan duct tape strips as far left as the first column will allow. Place another 16½" (42cm) strip of teal duct tape vertically to the right of the first column, as close as possible without overlapping.//

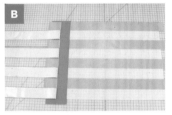

Replace the tan duct tape strips that were pulled back. This is the second column.

3 //**C** Repeat this process 10 more times—pulling back alternating tan duct tape strips, placing a teal duct tape strip, and replacing the tan duct tape strips—until you have 12 columns.//

4 Carefully flip the working fabric over so the parchment paper is facing up, again in the landscape position on the worktable. //**D** Gently peel off the paper, exposing the sticky side of the fabric.//

TO MAKE THE BACK SIDE OF THE FABRIC, //E place 11 strips of 26" (66cm) white heavy-duty duct tape vertically on top of the working fabric, overlapping the long edges of the strips by approximately ⅛" (3mm).//

5 You will now make the thin white strips in the tartan pattern. Flip the fabric over once more so the woven tan-and-teal front side faces up, again placing the fabric in the

landscape position. Cut a 24" (61cm) strip of white linen duct tape in half lengthwise. Cut each strip in half lengthwise again so you have 4 strips. The front side of the fabric is checkered with 8 rows and 12 columns. //**F** Starting at the top, place one of the white strips horizontally across the middle of the second, fourth, sixth, and eighth rows of the fabric.//

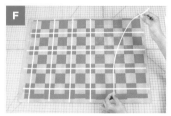

6 **TO MAKE THE THIN, DOUBLE ROSEWOOD STRIPS** in the pattern, cut 2 strips of 24" (61cm) Brazilian rosewood duct tape in half lengthwise. Cut each strip in half lengthwise again so you have 8 strips. Starting from the top row, place 2 side-by-side strips horizontally across the middle of the first, third, fifth, and seventh rows of the fabric.

7 Cut 3 strips of 17" (43cm) Brazilian rosewood duct tape in half lengthwise. Cut each strip in half lengthwise again so you have 12 strips. //**G** Starting at the far left strips, place 2 side-by-side strips vertically down the middle of the second, fourth, sixth, eighth, tenth, and twelfth columns of the fabric.//

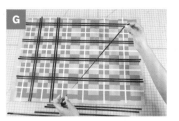

8 **TO MAKE THE OUTSIDE ROSEWOOD BORDER** of the bag, place a 25" (63.5cm) strip of Brazilian rosewood horizontally above the first row. The long bottom edge of the strip should slightly overlap the upper edge of the first row of tan and teal strips. Place a 25" (63.5cm) strip of Brazilian rosewood horizontally below the last row. The long upper edge of the strip should slightly overlap the bottom edge of the last row of tan and teal strips.

9 Place an 18" (45.5cm) strip of Brazilian rosewood vertically to the left of the first tan-and-teal column; the long right edge of the strip should slightly overlap the left edge of the column. //**H** Place another 18" (45.5cm) strip of Brazilian rosewood vertically to the right of the last tan-and-teal column; the long left edge of the strip should slightly overlap the right edge of the column.//

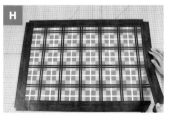

//**I** Cut through the middle of each Brazilian rosewood border, trimming the fabric to 17" × 25" (43cm × 63.5cm).//

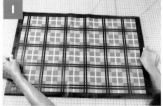

10 To make the side pieces of the bag, place the 7" × 8½" (18cm × 21.5cm) piece of parchment paper on the worktable. Make a duct tape fabric (see page 10) using 5 strips of 8" (20.5cm) white heavy-duty duct tape for the back side and 5 strips of 9½" (24cm) teal duct tape for the front side. Trim the fabric to 7" × 8½" (18cm × 21.5cm) high. //**J** Then cut the fabric vertically in half to make 2 smaller fabrics, each measuring 3½" × 8½" (9cm × 21.5cm). Set aside.//

11 Flip the main fabric over so the white duct tape side is facing up and place it in the portrait position. From the left corners, measure 1" (2.5cm)

(continued on next page)

inward along the top and bottom edges and lightly mark these 2 points with a grease pencil. //K Lightly draw a vertical line connecting the 2 marks. Starting from the top of this line, measure straight down 2¼" (5.5cm) and mark this point.//

12 Repeat step 11 on the right edge of the fabric.

13 To attach the sides to the main fabric, hold one of the side pieces in the portrait position, white duct tape side facing up. Place it on top of the main fabric along the left side of the vertical line you drew on the left. Align the top right corner of the side piece with the 2¼" (5.5cm) mark on the vertical line. Place an 8½" (21.5cm) strip of white heavy-duty duct tape vertically along the right edge of the side piece, connecting it to the main fabric. //L Attach the remaining side piece by repeating the above step on the vertical line you drew at the right side of the main bag.//

14 Place a 3½" (9cm) strip of white heavy-duty duct tape horizontally over the bottom edge of the left side piece. Be sure only half of the tape is on the side piece lengthwise. //M Fold it back so the sticky half is facing up. Pull the bottom edge of the side piece toward the main fabric. Align the side piece to the drawn line on the main fabric and stick the strip of white heavy-duty duct tape against the main fabric. Repeat this step to connect the right side piece.//

15 //N Place an 8½" (21.5cm) strip of white heavy-duty duct tape vertically along the remaining long edge of the left side piece. Be sure that only half of the strip is on the fabric lengthwise. Fold it back so the sticky half is facing up.//

Align the left edge of the side piece with the drawn vertical line of the main fabric.

//O Press down the strip of tape, connecting the side piece to the main fabric.//Repeat this step on the right side piece.

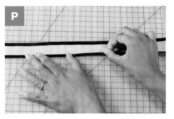

16 TO MAKE THE FIRST STRAP, //P cut a 28½" (72cm) strip of Brazilian rosewood duct tape and place it on the worktable with the sticky side facing up. Fold back both long edges approximately ¼" (6mm).//

Cut a 28½" (72cm) strip of white heavy-duty duct tape and trim the width to 1" (2.5cm). Stick the white duct tape strip lengthwise down the center of the Brazilian rosewood strip. Repeat for the second strap.

17 You will now attach the straps to the bag. //Q Starting from the top left corner of the front of the bag, measure 8½" (21.5cm) inward along the top edge and mark with a grease pencil.//

This is the vertical middle. Measure and mark 4" (10cm) to the right of this point along the top edge. From this new point, measure and mark 2" (5cm) straight down.

//**R** Cut a 1½" (3.8cm) horizontal slit into the bag starting at this point and cutting toward the right side of the bag. Repeat this step on the left side of the bag, starting from the middle point and measuring

4" (10cm) to the left, 2" (5cm) straight down, and then cutting a 1½" (3.8cm) horizontal slit into the bag from this point toward the left side of the bag.//

18 //**S** Insert 3" (7.5cm) of the ends of one of the straps into the slits.//

To create a more natural curve for the handle, slightly angle the straps in toward the vertical middle of the bag. Cover the end of each strap with a strip of 4½" (11.5cm) white duct tape on the inside of the bag.

19 //**T** Repeat step 18 to attach the second strap to the other side of the bag.//

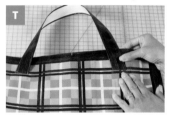

SPRINGTIME

This lovely satchel juxtaposes a pink camouflage with a classic mahogany print, mixing funk with functionality. As a pattern, pink camouflage seems counterintuitive. The purpose of camouflage is to conceal yourself for fighting or hunting. But how can you fight or hunt in a forest of pink flora and fauna? Who or what would you be fighting or hunting—fairies and unicorns? Pink camouflage is flower power: peace, love, and eternal springtime.

DUCT TAPE
white (heavy duty), 15 yd (13.7m)
pink camouflage, 12 yd (10.9m)
mahogany, 5 yd (4.6m)

ADDITIONAL MATERIALS
parchment paper, 20" × 12"
   (51cm × 30.5cm)
1½-gallon (1.89L) milk carton, rinsed, dried,
   and taken apart at the seams

TOOLS
• scissors
• craft knife
• metal ruler
• white grease pencil

1 For this project you will need 2 fabrics. Place the parchment paper on the worktable in the portrait position and make the first duct tape fabric (see page 10) using 12 strips of 13" (33cm) white duct tape for the back side and 8 strips of 21" (53.5cm) pink camouflage duct tape for the front side. Trim the fabric to 20" × 12" (51cm × 30.5cm). Repeat to make the second fabric.

2 **TO MAKE THE MAIN POCKET OF THE BAG,** place the fabrics on the worktable in the landscape position with the white duct tape side facing up. Place one fabric above the other so they are mirror images with a seam in the middle. Place a 20" (51cm) strip of white duct tape horizontally over the seam, connecting the two fabrics. Cut two 12" (30.5cm) strips of white duct tape. Starting from the top corners of the connected fabric, place 12" (30.5cm) strips of white duct tape vertically on both the right and left edges. Be sure that only half of each strip is on the fabric lengthwise. Fold back the tape strip on the left edge so the sticky half is facing up. **//A** Pull up the bottom left edge of the fabric so that it aligns with the top left edge of the fabric, folding at the middle seam. Press down the folded tape strip to secure the sides. Repeat with the tape strip on the right edge.**//**

3 //B To flatten the bottom of the bag, measure 2" (5cm) inward from both bottom corners along the bottom edge and mark with a grease pencil.//

Pinch each corner into a triangle. //C Fold the point of the triangle down and inward along the bottom of the bag, making a perpendicular line at the 2" (5cm) mark.//

//D Hold the corners in place with small pieces of white duct tape.//

4 TO MAKE THE FOLDS IN THE BAG, //E starting from the top left corner of the bag's front panel and moving along the top edge, measure every 4" (10cm) and mark with the grease pencil.//

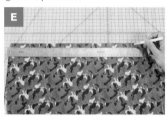

//F At each mark, make a ½" (13mm) vertical fold (using 1" of fabric) in the top edge. Hold each fold in place with a small piece of white duct tape on the back side of the fabric.//

5 Flip the bag over and repeat step 4 on the back panel.

6 To cover the seams, cut a 40" (101.5cm) strip of pink camouflage duct tape. //G Hold one end at the top left edge of the bag. Place the strip vertically down the left seam, across the bottom of the bag, and up the right seam until you reach the top edge of the bag.//Trim off any excess tape.

7 TO CREATE THE BAG'S MAHOGANY BOTTOM, cut a 23" (58.5cm) strip of mahogany duct tape and cut off the corners at each end in a curved line, rounding the edges. //H Center the strip lengthwise along the bottom of the bag. The ends of the strip should extend past the bottom and up the outer edges approximately 3" (7.5cm) on each side.//

8 **TO MAKE THE LIPS OF THE BAG,** cut 2 pieces from the milk carton that measure 14" × 3" (35.5cm × 7.5cm) each. Place the milk carton pieces in the landscape position on the worktable. Cut off the top corners of each piece in a curved line, rounding the edges. **//I** Cover one side of each piece with 2 strips of 15" (38cm) mahogany duct tape.**//**

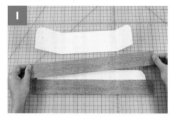

Trim off any excess tape. Flip each piece over and cover each piece with 2 strips of 15" (38cm) white duct tape. Trim off any excess tape.

9 **TO MAKE THE SLITS FOR THE STRAPS** to go through, place one bag lip on the worktable in the landscape position. From the bottom left corner, measure 2" (5cm) up along the left edge and mark it with a grease pencil. From this point, measure 2" (5cm) inward toward the right side and mark this point. Continuing to move inward from this point, cut a 1½" (3.8cm) horizontal line. On both the left and right ends of this line, measure and draw up

¼" (6mm) vertical lines. Draw a horizontal line connecting the bottom ends of the 2 vertical lines. You have now made a 1½" × ¼" (3.8cm × 6mm) rectangle. **//J** Cut out the rectangle.**//** Repeat on the right side.

10 Repeat step 9 on the other lip.

11 Flip the bag lips over so they are still in the landscape position but now with the white duct tape side facing up. Place a 14" (35.5cm) strip of white duct tape horizontally on the bottom edge of each lip. Be sure that only half of each lengthwise strip is on the bag lip. Place each lip on the top edges of the bag opening, the lip overlapping the top edge by approximately 1½" (3.8cm). Place the sticky part of the white tape strip on the lip's bottom edge inside the bag, pressing it to attach the lip.

12 **TO MAKE THE STRAPS,** cut a 26" (66cm) strip of white duct tape and a 26" (66cm) strip of mahogany duct

tape. Stick them together. Cut the width down to 1" (2.5cm). Repeat to make the second strap.

13 Insert 3" (7.5cm) of each end of one strap through the left and right slits on one side of the bag. Cover the ends of the strap with 4½" (11.5cm) strips of white duct tape on the inside of the bag.

14 **//K** Repeat step 13 with the other strap on the other side of the bag.**//**

REGATTA

The Regatta has a dynamic silhouette and a distinct pattern that attracts attention. White spheres set against a rich blue background are reminiscent of a bay dotted with sailboats, a scene both tranquil and vibrant. This satchel has a dual personality. It's got a mod vibe that you can pair with a baby-doll dress, but you can also prep it up with boat shoes and a chambray jumper. The choice is yours.

DUCT TAPE
white (heavy duty), 15 yd (13.7m)
dark blue, 11 yd (10m)
white (regular), 6 yd (5.5m)
white oak, 4 yd (3.7m)

ADDITIONAL MATERIALS
2 pieces of parchment paper, each measuring 18" × 13½" (45.5cm × 34.5cm)
printout of template (see page 199), trimmed to outline of shape

TOOLS
• scissors
• craft knife
• metal ruler
• graphite pencil
• white grease pencil
• circles inking template

1 For this project you will need 2 fabrics. Place the parchment paper on the worktable in the landscape position and make the first duct tape fabric (see page 10) using 11 strips of 14½" (37cm) white heavy-duty duct tape for the back side and 9 strips of 19" (48.5cm) dark blue duct tape for the front side. Trim the fabric to 18" × 13½" (45.5cm × 34.5cm). Repeat this step for the second fabric. Set the parchment paper aside.

2 **TO MAKE THE FRONT SIDE OF THE BAG,** place one of the fabrics on the worktable in the landscape position, dark blue duct tape side facing up. Place the template on the left side of the fabric. Disregarding the template's solid black curved column, use the grease pencil to trace the outside shape of the template onto the fabric. //**A** Flip the template from left to right and place the mirror-image template on the right side of the fabric, lining up the left edge of the template with the right edge of the tracing so that the line will be continuous. Trace the outside shape of the template again.// The full shape should have a curved top edge, curved outer edges, and a bottom edge that is narrower than the top edge. Cut out the shape from the fabric. Discard any extra fabric.

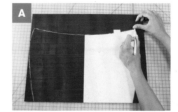

3 **TO MAKE THE BACK SIDE OF THE BAG,** repeat step 2 with the second fabric.

4 **TO MAKE THE CIRCLE STICKERS,** place one of the parchment paper pieces on the worktable in the landscape position. Use the circles inking template and graphite pencil to trace 34 circles with a diameter of 2½" (6.5cm) on the parchment paper. Cover one side of the parchment paper lengthwise with 11 strips of 14½" (37cm) white regular duct tape. **//B** The long edge of each strip should overlap the strip placed previously by approximately ¼" (6mm), creating a one-sided duct tape fabric on each parchment paper.**//**

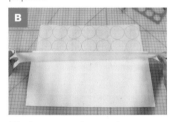

Flip it over so the parchment paper side is facing up. You will be able to see the tracings. **//C** Cut out all the circle shapes.**//**

5 Place one of the fabrics on the worktable. Along the bottom edge, measure and mark ½" (13mm), 4" (10cm), 7½" (19cm), 11"(28cm), and 14½" (37cm) in from the left corner going toward the right side. **//D** At these 5 marks draw vertical lines straight up the fabric with white grease pencil. Then start at the bottom of the ½" (13mm) vertical line. Measure up and mark 2" (5cm), 4" (10cm), 7" (18cm), and 10" (25.5cm). At these 4 marks draw horizontal lines across the fabric.**//**

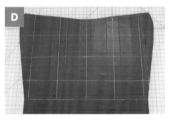

Along the second horizontal line from the top, place 5 circle stickers at the 5 points where the vertical lines intersect it. Place 4 circle stickers on the horizontal line above this row, and 4 circle stickers on the horizontal line below this row. The lines should go through the middle of each circle. **//E** Arrange 7 more circles along the top and outer edges, evenly spacing them to match the circles already on the fabric; the circles can extend past the outer edges of the fabric.**//**

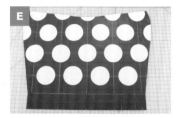

One by one, remove the parchment paper from the back of the circles and place them on the fabric. Trim off any excess duct tape around the edges of the fabric. Repeat this step on the second fabric.

6 **TO MAKE THE MAIN POCKET OF THE BAG,** place the fabrics on the worktable in the landscape position with the white heavy-duty duct tape side facing up. Place one fabric above the other so they are mirror images with the straight edges in the middle. **//F** Connect the 2 fabrics with a 14½" (37cm) strip of white heavy-duty duct tape over the seam.**//**

7 **//G** Starting from the top corners of the connected fabric, place a 14½" (37cm) strip of white heavy-duty duct tape vertically on the right and left edges. Be sure that only half of each strip is on the fabric lengthwise.**//** Fold back the

unattached tape strip on the left edge so the sticky half is facing up. Pull up the bottom left edge of the fabric so that it aligns with the top left edge of the fabric, folding at the middle seam. //**H** Press down the folded tape strip to secure the sides.// Repeat with the white tape strip on the right edge.

8 **TO MAKE THE STRAP STICKERS FOR THE FRONT AND BACK OF THE BAG,** place the second piece of parchment paper over the template. Trace the black strap outline twice. Flip the parchment paper over and place the blank side on the template. Trace the strap outline twice more. Set the template aside.

9 //**I** Cut 4 strips of 14½" (37cm) white heavy-duty duct tape.//

Cover a strap tracing on the parchment paper with one of the strips. Cut 4 strips of 14½" (37cm) white-oak duct tape. Place each strip lengthwise directly over a white heavy-duty duct tape strip on the parchment paper. Flip the parchment paper over. You should still be able to see your tracing. With scissors, cut out the strap stickers.

10 //**J** Use the template as a visual guide to attach the left strap stickers to the front and back of the bag.//

Peel off the parchment paper from the back of the strap stickers, but leave a 2" (5cm) piece of parchment on the top end of each strap sticker. The top ends of the strap stickers will extend past the bag opening. You will later attach a middle section to these strap extensions to create full bag straps.

11 Flip bag over and repeat step 10.

12 To flatten the bottom of the bag, //**K** measure 2" (5cm) inward along the bottom edge from both bottom corners and mark with a grease pencil.//

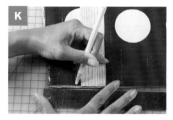

Pinch each corner into a triangle. Fold the point of the triangle down and inward along the bottom of the bag, making a perpendicular line at the 2" (5cm) mark. //**L** Hold the corners in place with small pieces of white heavy-duty duct tape.//

13 **TO MAKE THE MIDDLE SECTION OF THE STRAP,** cut a 16" (40.5cm) strip of white heavy-duty duct tape and a 16" (40.5cm) strip of white-oak duct tape. Stick them together. Cut the width down to 1" (2.5cm). Repeat this step to make a second middle section. Set aside.

14 Remove the parchment paper on the top of the left strap sticker already attached to the front bag. Cut a 6" (15cm) strip of heavy-duty white duct tape. //**M** Place the

(continued on next page)

white duct tape strip halfway lengthwise behind the left strap sticker so it extends past the top.//

Repeat for the remaining 3 strap stickers. //N Trim the width of each white duct tape strip to match the front side of the strap stickers, which should be 1" (2.5cm).//

15 On the front panel of the bag, line up the ends of the strap stickers with the ends of one of the middle sections of the strap from step 13. //O The white duct tape on the back side of the strap sticker should stick to the back side of the middle section.// Wrap 1" (2.5cm) strips of white-oak duct tape horizontally around the connecting seams.

16 Using the remaining middle section, repeat step 15 on the back of the bag.

17 TO MAKE THE TOGGLE CLOSURE, cut a 15" (38cm) strip of dark blue duct tape in half lengthwise. Roll the strips lengthwise to create 2 ropes.

18 Cut an 18" (45.5cm) strip of white-oak duct tape and set it on the worktable in a vertical position, white-oak side facing up. Along the top edge, measure and mark the center. From the bottom left corner, draw a diagonal line to the center mark just made. From the bottom right corner, draw a diagonal line to the center mark. You should now see a tall triangle with the base at the bottom of the strip. Cut the strip into this long triangle shape.

19 //P Flip the triangle strip over. Place one of the ropes from step 17 horizontally along the bottom edge of the white-oak triangle strip. Roll the triangle strip up over the rope, forming a bead.// Pull the ends of the rope behind the bead. Place a small piece of dark blue duct tape around the ends directly behind the bead.

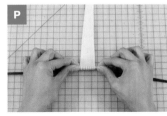

20 Mark the center of the top edge of the bag. From this point, measure 1½" (3.8cm) straight down, mark it with the grease pencil, and make a hole through both sides of the bag. //Q Push the ends of the rope attached to the bead through the front side of the bag and pull the rope until the bead is approximately 1" (2.5cm) from the front of the bag.// On the inside of the bag front, place a 4" (10cm) strip of white heavy-duty duct tape over the loose ends of the rope to secure it.

21 Flip the bag over to the back side. Fold the remaining dark blue duct tape rope in half. Push the ends through the hole made in step 20. Pull them through until there is approximately a 2" (5cm) loop. On the inside of the bag, place a 4" (10cm) strip of white heavy-duty duct tape over the loose ends of the rope to secure it.

KEMBERLY

The snakeskin facade of this modern bag can make you feel like you're living the high life. A real snakeskin satchel can cost hundreds or even thousands of dollars. This seemingly luxe satchel only *looks* expensive. You can make it for less than the cost of an extra-large cheese pizza!

DUCT TAPE
black (heavy duty), 15 yd (13.7m)
snakeskin, 10 yd (9.1m)

ADDITIONAL MATERIALS
parchment paper, 14" × 22"
   (35.5cm × 56cm)
parchment paper, 8" × 10"
   (20.5cm × 25.5cm)

TOOLS
• scissors
• craft knife
• metal ruler
• white grease pencil

1 Place the larger piece of parchment paper on the worktable in the portrait position and make a duct tape fabric (see page 10) using 14 strips of 15" (38cm) black duct tape for the back side and 8 strips of 23" (58.5cm) snakeskin duct tape for the front side. Trim the fabric to 14" × 22" (35.5cm × 56cm). Cut it horizontally into 2 pieces that measure 14" × 11" (35.5cm × 28cm) each.

2 Place the 2 fabrics on the worktable in the landscape position. //**A** Trim the top corners of each fabric in a curved line, rounding them. Set aside.//

3 **TO MAKE THE SIDES OF THE BAG,** using the smaller parchment paper, make a fabric using 6 strips of 11" (28cm) black duct tape for the back side and 8 strips of 9" (23cm) snakeskin duct tape for the front side. Trim the fabric to 8" × 10" (20.5cm × 25.5cm). Cut it vertically into 2 pieces that measure 4" × 10" (10cm × 25.5cm) each. Set aside.

4 **TO CREATE THE BOTTOM OF THE BAG,** make a fabric using 8 strips of 5" (12.5cm) black duct tape for the back side and 3 strips of 15" (38cm) snakeskin duct tape for the front side. Measure and trim the fabric to 14" × 4" (35.5cm × 10cm).

5 Place one of the fabrics in the landscape position on the worktable, black side facing up, rounded corners along the top edge. //**B** Place the bottom piece directly below the front piece in the landscape position, black side facing up. Line up the pieces so the horizontal edges touch and create seams. Place a 14" (35.5cm) strip of

black duct tape horizontally over the seam to connect the fabrics.//

Place the remaining fabric directly below the bottom piece in the landscape position, black side facing up, and rounded corners along the bottom edge. Line up the pieces so the horizontal edges touch and create seams. Place a 14" (35.5cm) strip of black duct tape horizontally over the seam to connect the fabrics.

6 Place a bag side vertically next to both the left and right edges of the bottom fabric, black sides facing up. The top edges of each bag side should align with the seam–between the bottom piece and bottom fabric. Line up the pieces so the vertical edges touch and create seams. //**C** Place a 10" (25.5cm) strip of black duct tape vertically over each seam to connect the bag sides to the bottom piece.//

7 //**D** Place a 4" (10cm) strip of black duct tape horizontally on the top edge of the left bag side. Be sure that only half of the strip is on the fabric lengthwise. Fold back the tape strip so the sticky half is facing up.//

Pull the top edge of the left bag side so that it aligns with the left edge of the bottom piece. Press down the folded tape strip to attach the left bag side to the bottom piece. //**E** Repeat this step on the top edge of the right bag side.//

8 Place a 10" (25.5cm) strip of black duct tape vertically over the left edge of the left bag side. Be sure that only half of the strip is on the fabric. //**F** Fold back the tape strip so the sticky half is facing up. Pull the left edge of the left bag side so that it aligns with the left edge of the top fabric. Press down the folded tape strip to attach the left bag side to the top fabric.//

Repeat this step on the top edge of the right bag side. The main pocket of the bag is done.

9 Place the bag flat on the worktable so the opening of the bag is at the top. Starting at the top corners, measure 1½" (3.8cm) downward along the left and right edges and mark these points with a grease pencil. //**G** Draw a horizontal line across the front bag connecting these 2 points.// Flip the bag over and repeat this step on the other side.

10 Position the bag so one of the bag sides is facing up. There should be marks along the left and right edges from step 9. //**H** Draw a horizontal line across the bag side connecting these 2 points.// Repeat this step on

the remaining bag side. All the horizontal lines should now be connected and go around the entire bag.

11 Repeat steps 9 and 10, but measure 2½" (6.5cm) down along the left and right edges. //**I** You should have a second horizontal line going around the entire bag.//

12 Place the bag flat on the worktable again so the opening of the bag is at the top. Starting from the left edge and moving to the right, measure along the top line you drew and mark the following measurements: ½" (13mm), 2½" (6.5cm), 3½" (9cm), 6½" (16.5cm), 7½" (19cm), 10½"

(26.5cm), 11½" (29cm), 13½" (34.5cm), 14½" (37cm), 15½" (39.5cm), 16½" (42cm), 17½" (44.5cm), 18½" (47cm), 20½" (52cm), 21½" (54.5cm), 28½" (72cm), 29½" (75cm), 31½" (80cm), 32½" (82.5cm), 33½" (85cm), 34½" (87.5cm), and 35½" (90cm). You will need to turn the bag as you measure and mark. //**J** From these points, draw a vertical line down to the the second line you drew. Cut slits at every drawn line.//

13 TO MAKE THE BELT, cut a strip of 20" (51cm) black duct tape and a strip of 20" (51cm) snakeskin duct tape. Stick them together. Cut the width down to ½" (13mm).

14 Starting from the outside at the 2½" (6.5cm) vertical slit on the front of the bag, weave the belt through the slits from left to right. //**K** Cinch the belt as you weave it through the bag sides only, which will cause the bags sides to have vertical folds between the slits.//

15 TO MAKE THE BUCKLE, cut a 3" (7.5cm) strip of black duct tape and fold it in half crosswise. //**L** Cut out 2 rectangles side by side that measure approximately ½" × 1" (13mm × 2.5cm) each.//

16 Wrap one end of the belt around the middle part of the buckle. Place a small piece of black duct tape on the end of the belt so it sticks to the back side. Loop the other end through the buckle. Trim the belt to 3" (7.5cm) past the buckle.

17 TO MAKE THE STRAPS, cut 2 strips of 26" (66cm) black duct tape and stick them together. Cut 2 strips, each with a width of ½" (13mm).

18 From the left and right upper corners of the front of the bag, measure 3" (7.5cm) inward along the upper edge and mark these points with a grease pencil on the inside of the bag. At these marks, place the ends of a strap inside the bag so they are 2½" (6.5cm) below the upper edge. Cover each strap end with a 3" (7.5cm) strip of black duct tape on the inside of the bag. Repeat this step on the back of the bag.

MESSENGER & FLAP BAG

I confess: I own at least fifteen messenger and flap bags, all of them made out of duct tape. The broad surface is a perfect place to express your visual imagination. The bag shape is fairly basic, and once you understand how to assemble the parts, it's easy to make over and over (and over) again. So this section is really about encouraging you to create your own stencils and stickers, essentially making a duct tape "painting" on a duct tape "canvas." Even if you have never painted in the traditional sense, don't worry: if you have parchment paper, a pencil, and a pair of (well-oiled) scissors, then you can paint with duct tape.

MONDRIAN

This bag is a hypnotic grid of primary colors that feels like it's moving. If you're familiar with the abstract painting *Broadway Boogie Woogie*, then the name "Mondrian" makes perfect sense for the design. But if video games are more your speed, then you would see *Minecraft* or *Space Invaders* as the source of inspiration. I like to believe that it can be both: a high-art-meets-pop-culture moment. Whatever the reason for tackling this bag, the result is a tapestry of colors that will dazzle the eyes.

DUCT TAPE
black (heavy duty), 17 yd (15.5m)
white, 5 yd (4.6m)
dark blue, 2 yd (1.8m)
red, 3 yd (2.7m)
yellow, 1 yd (0.9m)

ADDITIONAL MATERIALS
parchment paper, 14" × 18½"
 (35.5cm × 47cm)
parchment paper, 9½" × 18"
 (24cm × 45.5cm)
metal slider, 1½" (3.8cm) wide
magnetic snap closure, ¾" (2cm) diameter

TOOLS
• scissors
• craft knife
• metal ruler
• white grease pencil
• flat-nose pliers

1 Place the 14" × 18½" (35.5cm × 47cm) piece of parchment paper on the worktable in the landscape position and make a duct tape fabric (see page 10). You will work on the front of the fabric first, which is woven. Cut 4 strips of 19½" (49.5cm) black duct tape in half lengthwise. Cut those strips in half lengthwise again. You will have 16 strips with a width slightly less than ½" (13mm). Cut 3 strips of 19½" (49.5cm) white duct tape in half lengthwise. Cut those strips in half lengthwise again. You will have 12 strips with a width slightly less than ½" (13mm).

2 Starting at the top edge of the parchment paper, place 8 of the black duct tape strips horizontally, adding each strip directly below the one before it and leaving a hairline space between them. Next, place the 12 strips of white duct tape horizontally, adding each strip directly below the one before it and leaving a hairline space in between. //A Repeat with the other 8 strips of black duct tape.// The ends of all the strips should extend past the outer

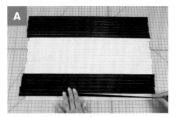

edges of the parchment paper by approximately ½" (13mm) and stick to the cutting mat below, which keeps the strips from sliding around.

3 Cut 4 strips of blue duct tape, 3 strips of red duct tape, and 2 strips of yellow duct tape, each 15" (38cm) long. Cut each in half lengthwise, then cut them in half lengthwise again. You will have 36 strips of various colors with a width slightly less than ½" (13mm).

4 **TO CREATE THE WEAVE,** pull back every other horizontal row of duct tape strips all the way to the left edge of the parchment paper. Be sure the strips remain sticking to the worktable just shy of the left edge of the parchment paper. **//B** Place a blue duct tape strip from step 3 on top of the black and white duct tape strips that are still flat on the paper, lining up the left long edge of the blue duct tape strip with the left edge of the parchment paper. Replace the duct tape strip rows that were pulled back. This is the first column.**//**

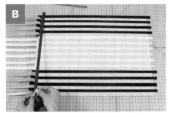

Pull back every other duct tape strip row of your choice as far

left as the first column will allow. You can stick to a mathematical pattern or pick arbitrarily. **//C** Place a red duct tape strip from step 3 to the right of the first blue duct tape strip, as close as possible without overlapping. Replace the duct tape strip rows that were pulled back.**//**

The color for the vertical columns is also your choice from this point on. **//D** Repeat this process 33 to 34 more times—pulling back duct tape strip rows, placing a duct tape strip from step 3 vertically, and replacing the duct tape strip rows—until you have covered the parchment paper with a woven fabric.**//**

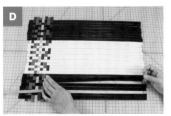

5 Carefully lift and flip the working fabric over so the parchment paper is facing up and in the landscape position. Gently peel off the parchment paper, exposing the sticky side of the fabric. Make the

back side by placing 11 strips of 15" (38cm) black duct tape vertically on top of the working fabric. The long edge of each strip should overlap the strip placed before it by approximately ⅛" (3mm), connecting them into one large piece.

6 Flip the fabric over so the woven fabric is facing up. At the left edge, place a 15" (38cm) strip of red duct tape vertically to the left of the first column of the weave, with the right long edge of the red tape slightly overlapping it. **//E** At the right edge of the fabric, place a 15" (38cm) strip of red duct tape vertically to the right of the last column of the weave, with the left long edge of the red tape slightly overlapping it.**//**

Trim the height of the fabric to 14" (35.5cm), which should coincide with the top and bottom edges of the weave. Trim the width of the fabric to 18½" (47cm), which should coincide with the outer long edges of the red duct tape strips.

7 Place the 9½" × 18" (24cm × 45.5cm) piece

(continued on next page)

of parchment paper on the worktable and make a second duct tape fabric (see page 10) using 11 strips of 10½" (26.5cm) black duct tape for the back side and 6 strips of 19" (49.5cm) white duct tape for the front side. Trim the fabric to 18" × 9½" (45.5cm × 24cm). Trim a piece off vertically that measures 4" × 9½" (10cm × 24cm) high. Set aside this smaller piece. The remaining fabric should measure 14" x 9½" (35.5cm × 24cm).

8 Place the second fabric on the worktable in the landscape position. Place the woven fabric above the second fabric in the portrait position. //F Flip both fabrics over so that the black duct tape sides of both fabrics are facing up, and the edges touch and create a middle seam.//

Place a 14" (35.5cm) strip of black duct tape over the seam, connecting the 2 fabrics.

9 TO MAKE THE BAG SIDES, cut the 4" × 9½" (10cm × 24cm) piece of fabric from step 7 into 2 pieces that measure 2" × 9½" (5cm × 24cm) each.

10 To attach the sides to the main bag, place one bag side each vertically along both the left and right edges of the bottom connected fabric so they touch, lining up the bottom edges and creating a seam between them. //G Cut 2 strips of 9½" (24cm) black duct tape and place a strip over each seam to connect the sides to the fabric.//

11 Cut 2 strips of 2" (5cm) black duct tape. Place a strip lengthwise over each bottom edge of the bag sides. Be sure that only half of the strips are on the fabric lengthwise. On the left bag side, fold the strip back so the sticky half is facing up. Align the bottom edge of the left bag side with the left edge of the main fabric. //H Press down the strip of tape, connecting the left bag side to the main fabric. Repeat this step on the right bag side.//

12 Place a strip of 9½" (24cm) black duct tape vertically along the remaining long edge of the left side piece. Be sure that only half of the strip is on the fabric lengthwise. Fold it back so the sticky half is facing up. //I Align the left edge of the side piece with the left edge of the main fabric. Press down the strip of tape, connecting the side piece to the main fabric.//

Repeat this step on the right side piece. The main bag is now complete.

13 TO MAKE A STRAP, cut a 32" (81cm) strip of white duct tape and place it on the worktable with the sticky side facing up. Fold back both long edges approximately ¼" (6mm). Cut a 32" (81cm) strip of black duct tape and trim it to 1" (2.5cm) wide. //J With the sticky side facing down, center the black duct tape strip lengthwise on top of the white duct tape strip.//

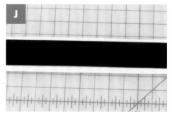

Repeat this step to make the second strap.

14 Starting from the top edge of the left bag side, measure down 1½" (3.8cm) along the left and right edges and mark these points. Draw a horizontal line with a white grease pencil connecting the 2 marks. Measure and mark ¼" (6mm) inward from each end of the drawn line and //**K** cut a 1½" (3.8cm) slit starting at each mark on the line.//

//**L** Insert the end of the first strap approximately 4" (10cm) into the slit.//

Attach the strap to the bag by placing a strip of 7" (18cm) black duct tape vertically over the strap end on the inside of the bag.

15 Repeat step 14 on the right bag side to attach the second strap. Loop a metal slider through the unattached end of the second strap, leaving a 1" (2.5cm) tail. Fold the tail over the middle bar of the slider and secure it with a 1" (2.5cm) strip of black heavy-duty duct tape. Weave the open end of the first strap through the slider.

16 //**M** Use 2 more strips of 4" (10cm) black duct tape to center and attach the magnetic snap closure ½" (13mm) from the edge of the flap (see page 12).//

17 The front and back sides are equally compelling, giving you flexibility on how you want to wear the bag—flap facing in or out.

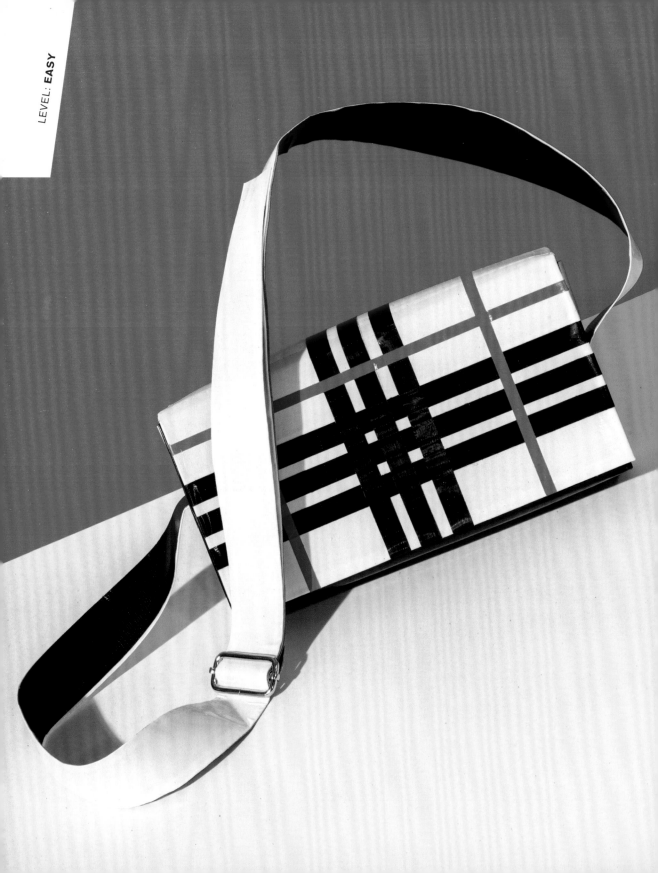

PUNK PLAID

This small flap bag is perfect for those late nights out dancing—or at a Green Day concert. Match this bag with jeans and a T-shirt for a casual yet put-together look, or with a solid-color mini dress for a more dressy ladies' night out.

DUCT TAPE
black (heavy duty), 10 yd (9.1m)
white, 4 yd (3.7m)
black (regular), 3 yd (2.7m)
red, 1 yd (0.9m)

ADDITIONAL MATERIALS
parchment paper, 9½" × 8½"
   (24cm × 21.5cm)
parchment paper, 9½" × 9½"
   (24cm × 24cm)
metal slider, 1½" (3.8cm) wide
magnetic snap closure, ¾" (2cm) diameter

TOOLS
• scissors
• craft knife
• metal ruler
• black grease pencil
• flat-nose pliers

1 Place the smaller parchment paper on the worktable in the portrait position and make a duct tape fabric (see page 10) using 6 strips of 9½" (24cm) black heavy-duty duct tape for the back side and 6 strips of 10½" (26.5cm) white duct tape for the front side. Trim the fabric to 9½" × 8½" (24cm × 21.5cm). Place the fabric in the landscape position on the worktable with the white duct tape side facing up.

2 **TO MAKE THE BLACK PLAID PATTERN,** cut 2 strips of 10" (25.5cm) black regular duct tape. Cut the strips into six 10" × ½" (25.5cm × 13mm) strips. Discard any extra tape. From the top and bottom left corners of the fabric, measure 4½" (11.5cm) inward and mark with a black grease pencil. Draw a vertical line connecting the 2 marks. **//A** Place one ½" (13mm) black regular duct tape strip vertically on the fabric, aligning the left long edge with the drawn line.**//**

A

Place a second ½" (13mm) black regular duct tape strip on the left side and a third on the right side of the first strip, with ¼" (6mm) space between them.

3 From the bottom edges of the fabric, measure 2" (5cm)

THE BOWLER HAT

I personally love the mod feel of a bowler hat paired with a gingham print. If you are a fan of the Surrealist René Magritte, then you'll think of his iconic hat-with-apple paintings. This bag is a wearable piece of art that will have many admirers doing a double-take and tipping their own chapeau to you.

DUCT TAPE
black (heavy duty), 20 yd (18.2m)
black-and-white gingham, 5 yd (4.6m)
white (regular), 2 yd (1.8m)
black (regular), 3 yd (2.7m)
sour apple linen Platypus Designer Duct Tape, 1 yd (0.9m)
mahogany Platypus Designer Duct Tape, 1½" (3.8cm)
white (heavy duty), 2 yd (1.8m)

ADDITIONAL MATERIALS
parchment paper, 9½" × 32½" (24cm × 82.5cm)
parchment paper, 5" × 9½" (12.5cm × 24cm)
printout of template (see page 200), trimmed to outline of shape
2 O-rings, 1½" (3.8cm) diameter
magnetic snap closure, ¾" (2cm) diameter

TOOLS
• scissors
• craft knife
• metal ruler
• graphite pencil
• white grease pencil
• flat-nose pliers

1 //**A** Place the larger parchment paper on the worktable in the portrait position and make a duct tape fabric (see page 10) using 19 strips of 10½" (26.5cm) black heavy-duty duct tape for the back side and 5 strips of 33½" (85cm) black-and-white gingham duct tape for the front side.//

Trim the fabric to 9½" × 32½" (24cm × 82.5cm). Set aside the parchment paper. (You will use it again in step 15.)

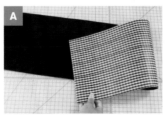

2 **TO MAKE THE BAG SIDES,** place the smaller parchment paper on the worktable in portrait orientation and make another duct tape fabric (see page 10) using 7 strips of 6" (15cm) black heavy-duty duct tape for the back side and 5 strips of 10½" (26.5cm) black-and-white gingham duct tape for the front side. Trim the fabric

to 5" × 9½" (12.5cm × 24cm). Cut the fabric into 2 pieces that measure 2½" × 9½" (6.5cm × 24cm) each.

3 Place the main fabric on the worktable in the portrait position, black heavy-duty duct tape side facing up. To attach the sides to the main bag, place one bag side vertically along both the left and right edges of the fabric so they touch, lining up the bottom edges and creating a seam between them. //B Cut 2 strips of 9½" (24cm) black heavy-duty duct tape and place a strip over each seam to connect the sides to the fabric.//

4 Cut 2 strips of 2½" (6.5cm) black heavy-duty duct tape. Place a strip lengthwise over each bottom edge of the bag sides. Be sure only half of each strip is on the fabric. //C On the left bag side, fold the strip back lengthwise so the sticky half is facing up.//

Align the bottom edge of the left bag side with the left edge of the main fabric. Press down the strip of tape, connecting the left bag side to the main fabric. //D Repeat this step on the right bag side.//

5 Place a strip of 9½" (24cm) black heavy-duty duct tape vertically along the remaining long edge of the left bag side piece. Again, be sure only half of the strip is on the fabric lengthwise. Fold it back so the sticky half is facing up. Align the left edge of the side piece with the left edge of the main fabric. //E Press down the strip of tape, connecting the side piece to the main fabric.//

Repeat with another strip of 9½" (24cm) black heavy-duty duct tape on the right side piece. The main pocket of the bag with a flap is now complete.

6 To cover the sides and bottom, cut a 28½" (72cm) strip of black regular duct tape. //F Starting at the top edge of one side of the bag, place this strip down the side, across the bottom, and up the other side.//

Cut a 28½" (72cm) strip of white regular duct tape and trim the width down to 1" (2.5cm). //G Starting at the top edge of one side of the bag and in the center of the black duct tape strip, place this strip down the side, across the bottom, and up the other side.//

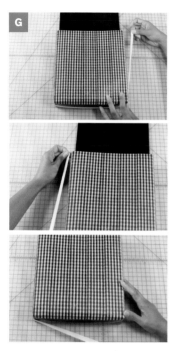

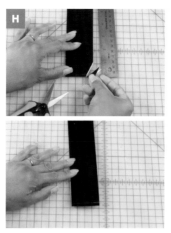

Repeat this step on the left side. //I When unfolded, the strap end should now have an hourglass shape.// Fold the other end of the strap and repeat this step.

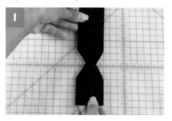

8 **TO MAKE THE STRAP LOOPS THAT WILL ATTACH TO THE O-RINGS,** //J cut a 20" (51cm) strip of black heavy-duty duct tape and a 20" (51cm) strip of white heavy-duty duct tape. Stick them together.//

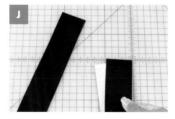

7 **TO MAKE THE MAIN STRAP,** cut a 36" (91cm) strip of black heavy-duty duct tape and a 36" (91cm) strip of white heavy-duty duct tape. Stick them together. Fold back one end approximately 3" (7.5cm), black side facing out, and rotate the strap so the folded edge is at the bottom. Starting at the right corner, measure ½" (13mm) inward along the folded edge and mark with a grease pencil. Starting again at the right corner, measure 1" (2.5cm) up the right side and mark with the pencil. //H Cut off the corner at a diagonal using these marks as the beginning and end points.//

Cut it in half to make 2 double-sided strips that measure 10" (25.5cm) each. Fold each of these pieces in half crosswise, black sides facing out.

9 Starting at the right corner of one of the folded pieces from step 8, measure ½" (13mm) inward along the folded edge and mark with a grease pencil. Starting again at the right corner, measure 1" (2.5cm) up the right side and mark with a grease pencil. Cut off the corner at a diagonal using these marks as the beginning and end points. Repeat this step on the left side. When unfolded, the strap loop should now have an hourglass shape.

10 Repeat step 9 on the other folded piece. Set them aside.

11 //K Refold the ends of the main strap through the O-rings. Secure the fold over the O-ring by placing a 1" (2.5cm) strip of white heavy-duty duct tape on each end, attaching it to the back side of the strap.//

(continued on next page)

BOWIE

Fuchsia and gold glitter can only mean one thing: glam rock! Strap this flap bag across your chest before heading to an Adam Lambert concert. Or if jamming out to "Space Oddity" at your local watering hole is more your thing, you can channel your best David Bowie while sporting his namesake carryall.

DUCT TAPE
white (heavy duty), 17 yd (15.5m)
fuchsia, 5 yd (4.6m)
gold chrome, 1 yd (0.9m)
gold glitter, 2" (5cm)

ADDITIONAL MATERIALS
parchment paper, 9½" × 33½"
    (24cm × 85cm)
parchment paper, 5" × 9½" (12.5 × 24cm)
printout of template (see page 203),
    trimmed to outline of shape
metal slider, 2" (5cm) wide
magnetic snap closure, ¾" (2.5cm) diameter

TOOLS
• scissors
• craft knife
• metal ruler
• graphite pencil
• white grease pencil
• circles inking template
• flat-nose pliers

1 **//A** Place the larger parchment paper on the worktable in the landscape position and make the main duct tape fabric (see page 10) using 5 strips of 34½" (87.5cm) white duct tape for the back side and 20 strips of 10½" (26.5cm) fuchsia duct tape for the front side.**//** Trim the fabric to 9½" × 33½" (24cm × 85cm).

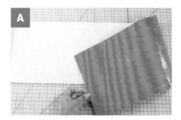

2 **TO MAKE THE BAG SIDES,** place the smaller parchment paper on the worktable in the portrait position and make another duct tape fabric using 7 strips of 6" (15cm) white duct tape for the back side and 5 strips of 10½" (26.5cm) fuchsia duct tape for the front side. Trim the fabric to 5" × 9½" (12.5cm × 24cm). Cut the fabric vertically into 2 pieces that measure 2½" × 9½" (6.5cm × 24cm) each. Set aside the parchment paper. (You will use it again in step 9.)

3 Place the main fabric on the worktable in the portrait position, white duct tape side

facing up. To attach the sides to the main bag, place one bag side vertically along both the left and right edges of the fabric so they touch, lining up the bottom edges and creating a seam between them. **//B** Cut 2 strips of 9½" (24cm) white duct tape and place a strip vertically over each seam to connect the sides

to the fabric.**//**

Place a 13½" (34.5cm) strip of gold chrome duct tape horizontally on the bottom edge so that only half of the tape is on the fabric lengthwise. Fold the other half of the strip over the bottom edge, creating a gold chrome border on both sides of the fabric.

4 Cut 2 strips of 2½" (6.5cm) white duct tape. Place a strip lengthwise over each bottom edge of the bag sides. Be sure that only half of the strips are on the fabric lengthwise. **//C** On the left bag side, fold the strip back so the sticky half is facing up.**//**

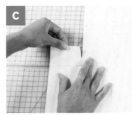

Align the bottom edge of the left bag side with the left edge of the main fabric. **//D** Press down the strip of tape, connecting the left bag side to the main fabric.**//** Repeat this step on the right bag side.

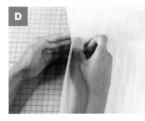

5 Place a strip of 9½" (24cm) white duct tape vertically along the remaining long edge of the left side piece. Be sure that only half of the strip is on the fabric lengthwise. Fold it back so the sticky half is facing up. Align the left edge of the side piece with the left edge of the main fabric. **//E** Press down the strip of tape, connecting the side piece to the main fabric.**//**

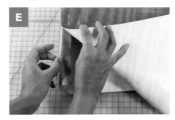

Repeat this step on the right side piece. The main pocket of the bag with flap is now complete.

6 **TO MAKE A STRAP,** cut a 30" (76cm) strip of white duct tape and a 30" (76cm) strip of fuchsia duct tape. Stick them together. Repeat this step to make the second strap.

7 Starting from the top edge of the left bag side, measure down 1½" (3.8cm) along the left and right edges and mark these points. Draw a horizontal line with a white grease pencil connecting the 2 marks. Measure ¼" (6mm) inward from each end of the drawn line and mark these points. **//F** Cut a 2" (5cm) line inward (toward the center), starting from the ¼" (6mm) mark made.**//**

//G Insert the end of the one strap approximately 4" (10cm) into the slit.**//**

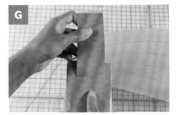

Attach the strap to the bag by placing 2 strips of 7" (18cm) white duct tape vertically over the strap end on the inside of the bag.

8 Repeat step 7 on the right bag side to attach the second strap. Loop a metal slider through the bottom end of the strap, leaving a 1" (2.5cm) tail. Fold the tail over the middle bar of the slider and secure it with a 1" (2.5cm) strip of dark blue duct tape. Weave the open end of the first strap through the slider.

9 Place the smaller parchment paper over the template. Be sure to leave room for another tracing in the next step. Trace the sun onto the parchment paper with a graphite pencil. Cover the tracing horizontally with 3 strips of 6" (15cm) gold chrome duct tape. Be sure

to overlap the long edges of each strip of gold chrome duct tape approximately ¼" (6mm). Flip over the parchment paper and you will be able to see the tracing. Using a pair of well-oiled scissors, cut out the sun, including the circle in the center. Set aside.

10 Place a 2" (5cm) strip of gold glitter tape on the parchment paper. //H Flip over the parchment paper and place the circles inking template on top, directly over the tape strip.//

Trace a 1⅝" (4cm) circle with a pencil onto the parchment paper. Cut out the circle with a pair of well-oiled scissors. Set aside.

11 Remove the parchment paper backing from the circle sticker and place it directly in the center of the bag flap.
//I Remove the parchment paper backing from the sun sticker and place it directly on top of the circle sticker.//

12 Use 2 strips of 4" (10cm) white duct tape to center and attach the magnetic snap closure ½" (13mm) from the edge of the flap (see page 12).

WHAM!

Mix a little Batman-style exclamation with a lot of Roy Lichtenstein pop-art sleekness, and you've got a messenger bag that really grabs people's attention. And if you happen to be a comic book fan, this bag will be ready to accompany you while perusing the stacks at your favorite comic shop.

DUCT TAPE
white (heavy duty), 17 yd (15.5m)
yellow, 5 yd (4.6m)
dark blue, 5 yd (4.6m)
black, 9 yd (8.2m)
white (regular), 2 yd (1.8m)
red, 2 yd (1.8m)

ADDITIONAL MATERIALS
parchment paper, 16½" × 19"
    (42cm × 48.5cm)
parchment paper, 13½" × 21½"
    (34.5cm × 57cm)
printout of template (see page 204),
    trimmed to outline of shape
metal slider, 2" (5cm) wide
magnetic snap closure, ¾" (2cm) diameter

TOOLS
• scissors
• craft knife
• metal ruler
• white grease pencil
• flat-nose pliers

1 Place the 16½" × 19" (42cm × 48.5cm) piece of parchment paper on the worktable in the landscape position and make a duct tape fabric (see page 10) using 10 strips of 20" (51cm) white heavy-duty tape for the back side and 7 strips of 17½" (44.5cm) yellow duct tape for the front side. Trim the fabric to 16½" × 19" (42cm × 48.5cm). (Save the parchment paper for step 14.)

2 Place the fabric on the worktable in the portrait position with the yellow duct tape side facing up. From the top and bottom left corners, measure 8¼" (21cm) toward the right and mark these points with a grease pencil. Draw a vertical line connecting these 2 marks. From the bottom corners of the fabric, measure up 4" (10cm) along the left and right edges and mark these points with a grease pencil.

//**A** Draw a horizontal line connecting the 2 marks.//

125

//**B** Starting at this line, place 2 strips of 17½" (44.5cm) dark blue duct tape horizontally across the center of the fabric.//

They will need to cross each other at the intersecting point of the drawn lines.

//**C** Starting at the drawn vertical line, place 2 strips of 20" (51cm) dark blue duct tape vertically down the fabric.// They will need to cross each other at the same intersecting point as the previous pair of dark blue duct tape strips.

3 Cut a 23" (58.5cm) strip of dark blue duct tape. //**D** Place it diagonally on the fabric starting from the bottom right corner.//

It should go over the point where the strips from step 2 intersect, and past the opposite edge. Trim the excess tape along the edges of the main fabric.

4 Cut another 23" (58.5cm) strip of dark blue duct tape. //**E** Place it diagonally on the fabric starting from the bottom left corner.//

It should go over the point where the strips from step 2 intersect, and past the opposite edge. Trim off the excess blue tape along the edges of the fabric. Set the fabric aside.

5 Place the 21½" × 13½" (54.5cm × 34.5cm) piece of parchment paper on the worktable in the portrait position and make a second duct tape fabric (see page 10) using 15 strips of 14½" (37cm) white heavy-duty duct tape for the back side and 9 strips of 22½" (57cm) black duct tape for the front side. Trim the fabric to 21½" × 13½" (54.5cm × 34.5cm). Trim a piece off vertically that measures 5" × 13½" (12.5cm × 34.5cm). Set aside the smaller piece. The remaining fabric should measure 16½" × 13½" (42cm × 34.5cm).

6 Place the yellow-and-blue fabric on the worktable in the portrait position, colorful side facing up. The intersecting blue duct tape strips should be on the top portion of the fabric. Flip the fabric over so the white heavy-duty duct tape side is facing up, making sure to keep the blue strips at the top. Place the black-and-white fabric directly below it, white heavy-duty duct tape side facing up, in the landscape position so that the edges touch and create a middle seam. //**F** Place a 16½" (42cm) strip of white heavy-duty duct tape over the seam, connecting the 2 fabrics.//

7 **TO MAKE THE BAG SIDES,** cut the 5" × 13½" (12.5cm × 34.5cm) piece of fabric from step 5 into 2 pieces that measure 2½" × 9½" (6.5cm × 24cm) high. Discard any extra duct tape.

8 To attach the sides to the main bag, place one bag side vertically along both the left and right edges of the bottom connected fabric so they touch,

lining up the bottom edges and creating a seam between them. Be sure the white heavy-duty duct tape sides are facing up. //G Cut 2 strips of 9½" (24cm) white heavy-duty duct tape and place a strip over each seam to connect the sides to the fabric.//

9 Cut 2 strips of 2½" (6.5cm) white heavy-duty duct tape. Place a strip lengthwise over each bottom edge of the bag sides. Be sure that only half of the strips are on the fabric lengthwise. On the left bag side, fold the strip back so the sticky half is facing up. Align the bottom edge of the left bag side with the left edge of the main fabric. Press down the strip of tape, connecting the left bag side to the main fabric. Repeat this step on the right bag side.

10 //H Place a strip of 9½" (24cm) white heavy-duty duct tape vertically along the remaining long edge of the left side piece.//

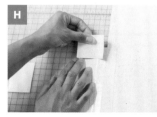

Be sure that only half of the strip is on the fabric lengthwise. Fold it back so the sticky half is facing up. //I Align the left edge of the side piece with the left edge of the main fabric. Press down the strip of tape, connecting the side piece to the main fabric.//

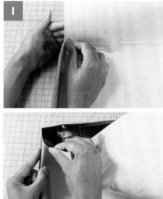

Repeat this step on the right side piece. The main bag is now complete.

11 TO MAKE A STRAP, cut a 32" (81cm) strip of black regular duct tape and a 32" (81cm) strip of white heavy-duty duct tape. Stick them together. Repeat this step for the second strap.

12 Starting from the top edge of the left bag side, measure down 1½" (3.8cm) along the left and right edges and mark these points. Draw a horizontal line with a white grease pencil connecting the 2 marks. Measure ¼" (6mm)

inward from each end of the drawn line and mark these points. //J Cut a 2" (5cm) line inward (toward the center), starting from the ¼" (6mm) mark made.//

//K Insert approximately 4" (10cm) of the end of the first strap into the slit.//

Attach the strap to the bag by placing 2 strips of 7" (18cm) white heavy-duty tape vertically over the strap end on the inside of the bag.

13 Repeat step 12 on the right bag side to attach the second strap. Loop a metal slider through the unattached end of the second strap, leaving a 1" (2.5cm) tail. Fold the tail over the middle bar of the slider and secure it with a 1" (2.5cm) strip of white heavy-duty duct tape. Weave the open end of the first strap through the slider.

(continued on next page)

14 Place the left side of the 13½" × 21½" (34.5cm × 54.5cm) parchment paper over the template. (Be sure to leave space for more tracings in steps 15–17.) Trace the cloud with a graphite pencil onto the parchment paper. Horizontally cover the tracing with 5 strips of 12" (30.5cm) white regular duct tape. Be sure to overlap the long edges of each strip of white regular duct tape approximately ¼" (6mm). Flip over the parchment paper and you will be able to see the tracing. Using a pair of well-oiled scissors, cut out the cloud. Set aside.

15 Use the same parchment paper from step 14 and place it over the template. (Be sure to leave space for more tracings in steps 16 and 17.) Trace the word bubble with a graphite pencil onto the parchment paper. Cover the tracing horizontally with 5 strips of 11" (28cm) red duct tape, one long edge of each strip overlapping the previously placed strip by approximately ¼" (6mm). Flip over the parchment paper and you will be able to see the tracing. Using a pair of well-oiled scissors, cut out the word bubble. Set aside.

16 Use the same parchment paper from step 15 and place it over the template. (Be sure to leave space for more tracings in step 17.) Trace the

word *WHAM!* with a graphite pencil onto the parchment paper. Cover the tracing horizontally with 3 strips of 11" (28cm) black duct tape, one long edge of each strip overlapping the previously placed strip by approximately ¼" (6mm). Flip over the parchment paper and you will be able to see the tracing. Using a pair of well-oiled scissors, cut out the *WHAM!* letters individually. Set aside.

17 Place the same parchment paper from step 16 over the template. Trace the word *WHAM!* again with a graphite pencil onto the parchment paper. Cover the tracing horizontally with 3 strips of 11" (28cm) white regular duct tape. Be sure to overlap the long edges of each strip approximately ¼" (6mm). Flip over the parchment paper and you will be able to see the tracing. //L Using a pair of well-oiled scissors, cut out the *WHAM!* letters individually. Set aside.//

18 You will now assemble the stickers onto the cloud sticker, using the template

as a placement guide. Remove the parchment-paper backing from the word-bubble sticker and place it directly in the center of the cloud. Remove the parchment-paper backing from the black duct tape *WHAM!* stickers and place them on top of the word bubble. //M Remove the parchment-paper backing from the white duct tape *WHAM!* stickers and place them on top and slightly to the left of the black *WHAM!* letters.//

19 //N Remove the parchment paper backing from the cloud sticker and place it on the center of the bag flap, directly over the section where the dark blue duct tape strips intersect.//

20 Use 2 strips of 4" (10cm) white heavy-duty duct tape to center and attach the magnetic snap closure ½" (13mm) from the edge of the flap (see page 12).

MOVEMENT UNDERGROUND

You can draw inspiration from the subterranean transportation lines of Paris, London, Tokyo, or New York City. In addition to helping you navigate the transit system, subway maps are designed to be aesthetically pleasing, with boldly colored lines that harmoniously intersect and form geometric shapes. Movement Underground takes the subway map motif and elevates it to a fashion statement.

DUCT TAPE

white (heavy duty), 17 yd
(15.5m)
white linen, 5 yd (4.6m)
green, 9 yd (8.2m)
orange, 1 yd (0.9m)
purple, 1 yd (0.9m)
yellow, 1 yd (0.9m)
dark blue, 1 yd (0.9m)
dark green, 1 yd (0.9m)

ADDITIONAL MATERIALS

parchment paper, 16½" × 19"
(42cm × 48.5cm)
parchment paper, 13½" × 21½"
(34.5cm × 54.5cm)
metal slider, 2" (5cm) wide
magnetic snap closure, ¾"
(2cm) diameter

TOOLS

• scissors
• craft knife
• metal ruler
• white grease pencil
• flat-nose pliers

1 Place the 16½" × 19"
(42cm × 48.5cm) piece
of parchment paper on the
worktable in the landscape
position and make a duct tape
fabric (see page 10) using
10 strips of 20" (51cm) white
heavy-duty duct tape for the
back side and 7 strips of 17½"
(44.5cm) white linen duct
tape for the front side. Trim the
fabric to 16½" × 19" (42cm ×
48.5cm).

2 Place the 13½" × 21½"
(34.5cm × 54.5cm) piece
of parchment paper on the
worktable in the portrait position
and make a second duct tape

fabric using 15 strips of 14½"
(37cm) white heavy-duty duct
tape for the back side and 9
strips of 22½" (57cm) green
duct tape for the front side.
Trim the fabric to 21½" × 13½"
(54.5cm × 34.5cm). Trim off a
piece vertically that measures
5" × 13½" (12.5cm × 34.5cm).
Set aside the smaller piece. The
remaining fabric should measure
16½" × 13½" (42cm × 34.5cm)
high.

3 Place the fabric from step 1
on the worktable in the
portrait position with the white
heavy-duty duct tape side facing
up. Place the green and white
heavy-duty duct tape fabric from
step 2 directly below it, white
heavy-duty duct tape side facing
up, in the landscape position
so that the 16½" (42cm) edges
touch and create a middle
seam. **//A** Place a 16½" (42cm)
strip of white heavy-duty duct
tape horizontally over the seam,
connecting the 2 fabrics.**//**

4 **TO MAKE THE BAG SIDES,**
cut the 5" × 13½" (12.5cm
× 34.5cm) piece of fabric
from step 2 into 2 pieces that
measure 2½" × 9½" (6.5cm ×
24cm) each. Discard any extra
duct tape.

5 To attach the sides to the
main bag, place one bag
side each vertically along both
the left and right edges of the
bottom connected fabric so
they touch, lining up the bottom
edges and creating a seam
between them. **//B** Cut 2 strips
of 9½" (24cm) white heavy-duty
duct tape and place a strip over
each seam to connect the sides
to the fabric.**//**

6 Cut 2 strips of 2½" (6.5cm)
white heavy-duty duct tape.
Place a strip lengthwise over
each bottom edge of the bag
sides. Be sure that only half
of the strips are on the fabric
lengthwise. **//C** On the left bag
side, fold the strip back so the
sticky half is facing up.**//**

Align the bottom edge of the left
bag side with the left edge of
the main fabric. **//D** Press down
the strip of tape, connecting the
left bag side to the main fabric.
Repeat this step on the right
bag side.**//**

7 Place a strip of 9½" (24cm) white heavy-duty duct tape vertically along the remaining long edge of the left side piece. Be sure that only half of the strip is on the fabric lengthwise. Fold it back so the sticky half is facing up. Align the left edge of the side piece with the left edge of the main fabric. **//E** Press down the strip of tape, connecting the side piece to the main fabric.**//**

Repeat this step on the right side piece. The main bag is now complete.

8 **TO MAKE A STRAP,** cut a 32" (81cm) strip of white heavy-duty duct tape and a 32" (81cm) strip of green duct tape. Stick them together. Repeat this step to make the second strap.

9 Starting from the top edge of the left bag side, measure down 1½" (3.8cm) along the left and right edges and mark.

Draw a horizontal line with a white grease pencil connecting the 2 marks. Measure and mark ¼" (6mm) inward from each end of the drawn line. **//F** Cut a 2" (5cm) line inward (toward the center), starting from the ¼" (6mm) mark made.**//**

//G Insert approximately 4" (10cm) of the end of the first strap into the slit.**//**

Attach the strap to the bag by placing 2 strips of 7" (18cm) white heavy-duty duct tape vertically over the strap end on the inside of the bag.

10 Repeat step 9 on the right bag side to attach the second strap. Loop a metal slider through the unattached end of the second strap, leaving a 1" (2.5cm) tail. Fold the tail over the middle bar of the slider and secure it with a 1" (2.5cm) strip of white heavy-duty duct tape. Weave the open end of the first strap through the slider.

11 **TO MAKE THE SUBWAY GRID PATTERN,** cut one 17½" (44.5cm) strip each from orange, purple, yellow, dark blue, and dark green duct tape. Cut 3 strips lengthwise from each color; each strip is approximately ¼" (6mm) wide. **//H** Place these strips across the front side of the bag flap in a grid or a pattern that is similar to a subway map, where a single color represents a transportation line.**//**

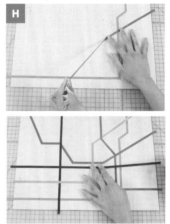

Be sure to crisscross some strips. Trim or fold over any extra duct tape that extends beyond the edges of the flap.

12 Use 2 strips of 4" (10cm) white heavy-duty duct tape to center and attach the magnetic snap closure ½" (13mm) from the edge of the flap (see page 12).

CARIBBEAN DREAM

What's more relaxing than a sunset on the beach? This messenger bag evokes that perfect sky after the sun has melted into the ocean, leaving an aura of red, orange, and yellow—and cold cocktails served with speared fruit and paper umbrellas. Use this bag to pack your essentials for a quick weekend getaway, and soon those visions will become a reality.

DUCT TAPE
black (heavy duty), 17 yd (15.5m)
red, 5 yd (4.6m)
orange, 1 yd (0.9m)
gold chrome, 1 yd (0.9m)
yellow, 4 yd (3.7m)
black (regular), 9 yd (8.2m)

ADDITIONAL MATERIALS
parchment paper, 16½" × 19"
    (42cm × 48.5cm)
parchment paper, 13½" × 21½"
    (34.5cm × 54.5cm)
printout of palm tree template (see page 204),
    trimmed to outline of shape
metal slider, 2" (5cm) wide
magnetic snap closure, ¾" (2cm) diameter

TOOLS
• scissors
• craft knife
• metal ruler
• white grease pencil
• flat-nose pliers

1 Place the 16½" × 19" (42cm × 48.5cm) piece of parchment paper on the worktable in the portrait position and make a duct tape fabric (see page 10) using 10 strips of the 20" (51cm) black heavy-duty duct tape for the back side.

2 **TO MAKE THE FRONT SIDE**, start at the top and place 7 strips of 17½" (44.5cm) red duct tape. Be sure to overlap the long edges of each strip approximately ¼" (6mm). Add the remaining strips, continuing to overlap the long edges, to the front side in the following order: **//A** 1 strip of 17½" (44.5cm) orange duct tape, 1 strip of 17½" (44.5cm) gold chrome duct tape, 2 strips of 17½" (44.5cm) yellow duct tape, and 1 strip of 17½" (44.5cm) black regular duct tape. Trim this fabric to 16½" × 19" (42cm × 48.5cm).**//**

3 Place the 13½" × 21½" (34.5cm × 54.5cm) piece of parchment paper on the worktable and make a second duct tape fabric using 15 strips of 14½" (37cm) black heavy-duty duct tape for the back side and 9 strips of 22½" (57cm) black regular duct tape for the front side. Trim the fabric to 21½" × 13½" (54.5cm × 34.5cm) high. Trim off a piece vertically that measures 5" × 13½" (12.5cm × 34.5cm). Set aside the smaller piece. The remaining fabric should measure 16½" × 13½" (42cm × 34.5cm).

4 Place the multicolored fabric on the worktable in the portrait position with the front side facing up. The red duct tape strips should be on the bottom portion of the fabric. Flip the fabric over so the black heavy-duty duct tape side is facing up. Place the other fabric directly below it, black heavy-duty duct tape side facing up, in the landscape position so that the edges of both pieces touch and create a middle seam. **//B** Place a 16½" (42cm) strip of black heavy-duty duct tape horizontally over the seam, connecting the 2 fabrics.**//**

5 **TO MAKE THE BAG SIDES,** cut the 5" × 13½" (12.5cm × 34.5cm) piece of fabric from step 3 into 2 pieces that measure 2½" × 9½" (6.5cm × 24cm) each. Discard any extra duct tape.

6 To attach the sides to the main bag, place one bag side vertically along both the left and right edges of the bottom connected fabric so they touch, black sides facing up, lining up the bottom edges and creating a seam between them. **//C** Cut 2 strips of 9½" (24cm) black heavy-duty tape and place a strip vertically over each seam to connect the sides to the main bag fabric.**//**

7 Cut 2 strips of 2½" (6.5cm) black heavy-duty duct tape. Place a strip lengthwise over each bottom edge of the bag sides. Be sure that only half of the strips are on the fabric lengthwise. **//D** On the left bag side, fold the strip back so the sticky half is facing up.**//**

//E Align the bottom edge of the left bag side with the left edge of the main fabric. Press down the strip of tape, connecting the left bag side to the main fabric.**//**

//F Repeat this step on the right bag side.**//**

8 Place a strip of 9½" (24cm) black heavy-duty duct tape vertically along the remaining long edge of the left side piece. Be sure that only half of the strip is on the fabric lengthwise. Fold it back so the sticky half is facing up. **//G** Align the left edge of the side piece with the

left edge of the main fabric. Press down the strip of tape, connecting the side piece to the main fabric.//

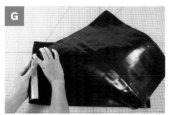

Repeat this step on the right side piece. The main bag is now complete.

9 **TO MAKE A STRAP,** cut a 32" (81cm) strip of black heavy-duty duct tape and a 32" (81cm) strip of yellow duct tape. Stick them together. Repeat this step to make the second strap.

10 Starting from the top edge of the left bag side, measure down 1½" (3.8cm) along the left and right edges and mark these points. Draw a horizontal line with a white grease pencil connecting the 2 marks. Measure ¼" (6mm) inward from each end of the drawn line and mark these points. //**H** Cut a 2" (5cm) slit between each mark on the line.//

//I Insert the end of the first strap approximately 4" (10cm) into the slit.//

Attach the strap to the bag by placing 2 strips of 7" (18cm) black heavy-duty duct tape vertically over the strap end on the inside of the bag.

11 Repeat step 10 on the right bag side to attach the second strap. Loop a metal slider through the unattached end of the second strap, leaving a 1" (2.5cm) tail. Fold the tail over the middle bar of the slider and secure it with a 1" (2.5cm) strip of black heavy-duty duct tape. Weave the open end of the first strap through the slider.

12 Place the smaller parchment paper over the template. //**J** Trace the palm tree onto the parchment paper with a pencil.//

Cover the tracing with 5 strips of 7" (18cm) black regular duct tape. Be sure to overlap the black duct tape strips at the long edges by approximately ¼" (6mm). Flip over the parchment paper and you will be able to see the tracing. Using a pair of well-oiled scissors, cut out the palm tree. Discard any extra tape and parchment paper.

13 //**K** Remove the parchment-paper backing from the palm tree sticker and place the sticker directly in the center of the bag flap.//

14 //**L** Use 2 strips of 4" (10cm) black heavy-duty duct tape to center and attach the magnetic snap closure ½" (13mm) from the edge of the flap (see page 12).//

TOTE

There's no question about it—totes are everywhere. Whether the high-end leather versions or their canvas counterparts found at grocery store checkout counters, totes are a mark not only of our fast-paced lives, but also the conservation-conscious world we live in. I know of at least two chain clothing stores that wrap up your purchases in a sack made of recycled materials—which you can then reuse again and again.

When made from duct tape, a tote is more than a tote. It's an UBER tote, the best of both worlds. It's strong, waterproof, and long-lasting, and easily repaired—just add more duct tape! And it's also just as stylish as the trendy models.

E.L.F.

Named after a fellow baseball mom who expertly sits in a fold-up stadium chair with style, this tote has the capacity to hold all the little things that one needs to survive on the sidelines, which may or may not include an extra nonfat latte and mini iPad. But this snazzy bag is not just for baseball moms. The rich red and white linen stripes have a wide appeal.

DUCT TAPE
white (heavy duty), 13 yd (11.8m)
white linen (Platypus brand), 5 yd (4.6m)
red, 6 yd (5.5m)
Brazilian rosewood (Platypus brand), 1yd (0.9m)

ADDITIONAL MATERIALS
parchment paper, 17" × 12" (43cm × 30.5cm)
parchment paper, 13" × 4" (33cm × 10cm)
printout of template (see page 204), trimmed to outline of shape

TOOLS
• scissors
• craft knife
• metal ruler
• grease pencil

1 For this project you will need 2 fabrics. Place the larger parchment paper on the worktable in the portrait position and begin making the first duct tape fabric (see page 10) using 10 strips of 13" (33cm) white heavy-duty duct tape for the back side. Flip the working fabric over. Without removing the parchment paper, trim the working fabric to 17" × 12" (43cm × 30.5cm). Place it on the worktable in the landscape position with the parchment paper facing up. Remove the parchment paper.

2 **TO MAKE THE STRIPED FRONT SIDE OF THE FABRIC,** cut a strip of 18" (45.5cm) white linen duct tape and place it on the worktable with the sticky side facing up. Fold back one of the long edges approximately ¼" (6mm). Flip the strip over so the sticky side is facing down and the folded edge is at the bottom. **//A** Hold it horizontally over the fabric from step 1. Align the folded edge of the strip with the bottom edge of the fabric and carefully place the strip down.**//**

A

Cut another strip of 18" (45.5cm) white linen duct tape and hold it horizontally above the first strip, sticky side facing down. //B Carefully place the strip down so the bottom overlaps the top of the first strip by approximately ⅛" (3mm).//

3 Cut a strip of 18" (45.5cm) red duct tape and place it on the worktable with the sticky side facing up. Fold back one of the long edges approximately ¼" (6mm). Flip the strip over so the sticky side is facing down and the folded edge is at the bottom. //C Hold it horizontally and carefully place the strip so the folded edge overlaps the top edge of the white linen strip by approximately ¹⁄₁₆" (1.5mm).//

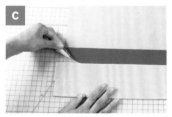

Cut another strip of 18" (45.5cm) red duct tape and hold it horizontally above the first red strip, sticky side facing down.

//D Carefully place the strip down so the bottom edge overlaps the top of the first red strip by approximately ⅛" (3mm).//

4 Repeat step 3 with 2 strips of 18" (45.5cm) white linen duct tape. //NOTE: Platypus tape is thicker than other brands of duct tape. Folds in the duct tape will eventually unfold, so be sure the folded edge is not overlapping a strip of tape any more than ¹⁄₁₆" (1.5mm). This will ensure that the folds will adhere to the sticky side of the strips on the sticky side of the working fabric.)//

5 Repeat step 3 with 2 strips of 18" (45.5cm) red duct tape. //E The top strip should extend past the top edge of the fabric by approximately ½" (13mm). Fold this section of strip over the top edge.//

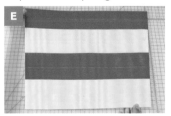

6 Trim the left and right edges so the front side of the fabric is the same width as the back side. The overall size of the fabric should now be 17" × 12" (43cm × 30.5cm).

7 Starting from the bottom left corner, measure 1¼" (3cm) inward along the bottom edge and mark with a grease pencil. Starting from the bottom right corner, measure 1¼" (3cm) inward along the bottom edge and mark with a grease pencil. //NOTE: Line up the metal ruler diagonally between the top left corner and the 1¼" (3cm) mark on the bottom left.// With a craft knife, cut off the fabric on the left side of the ruler. Line up the metal ruler diagonally between the top right corner and the 1¼" (3cm) mark on the bottom right. With a craft knife, cut off the fabric on the right side of the ruler. You should now have a trapezoid-shaped fabric with a top edge measuring 17" (43cm) and a bottom edge measuring 14½" (37cm).

8 To make the second fabric, repeat steps 1–7.

9 Place the fabrics on the worktable side by side with the white duct tape side facing up, creating a vertical seam in the middle. Place a 12" (30.5cm) strip of white

(continued on next page)

LIFE IS A BEACH

This loosely "woven" duct tape tote is large enough to fit all your summer essentials and then some! Throw in a towel, sunglasses, water bottle, volleyball, flip-flops, and (of course) tons of sunblock, and head to the nearest beach. The loose weave allows you to toss your stuff back in even if it's wet—remember, duct tape is waterproof. So a wet bathing suit and sopping towel are never a problem and sand stays at the beach after you head home.

DUCT TAPE
blue, 22 yd (20m)
green, 16 yd (14.5m)
orange, 5 yd (4.6m)

TOOLS
• scissors
• craft knife
• metal ruler
• white grease pencil

1 Cut 2 strips of 18" (45.5cm) blue duct tape. Stick them together. Repeat 7 times until you have 8 blue double-sided strips.

2 Repeat step 1 using 16 strips of 18" (45.5cm) green duct tape. You now have 8 green double-sided strips.

3 Set aside 4 blue and 4 green double-sided strips. Arrange the remaining double-sided strips in horizontal rows across your worktable approximately ½" (13mm) apart from each other. Be sure to alternate the colors.

4 //A Cut a strip of 21" (53.5cm) blue duct tape and place it vertically down the left side of the rows, approximately ½" (13mm) in from the left edge of each row.

Cut a strip of 21" (53.5cm) green duct tape and place it vertically approximately ½" (13mm) to the right of the blue strip. Repeat this step until you have 7 columns.// The last column should be blue.

5 Carefully lift the strips and flip the working fabric over from left to right. The sticky side of the duct tape columns should be facing up. //B Carefully cover the columns with 21" (53.5cm) strips of duct tape in the same color to make a faux woven duct tape fabric.//

Trim the outer edges of the fabric to align with the outermost rows and columns. The trimmed fabric should be approximately 20" × 17" (51cm × 43cm).

6 //C Repeat steps 1–5 to make the second fabric.//

7 Place the fabrics on the worktable in the landscape position with two 20" (51cm) edges touching and create a middle seam.

8 //D Connect the fabrics together by placing a strip of 20" (51cm) blue duct tape horizontally over the seam.//

9 //E Starting from the top corners of the connected fabric, place a strip of 17" (43cm) blue duct tape vertically on both the left and right edges of the connected fabric.//

Be sure that only half of each strip is attached to the fabric lengthwise.

10 //F On the left edge, fold back the tape strip so the sticky half is facing up.//

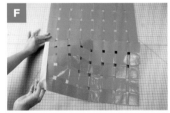

Pull up the bottom of the connected fabric and fold it horizontally at the middle seam. It should completely cover the top of the fabric. //G Line up the left edges and press down the folded tape strip to secure the seams. Repeat on the right edge.//

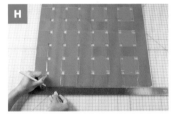

11 To flatten the bottom of the bag, //H measure 2" (5cm) inward from each corner along the bottom edge and mark with a grease pencil.//

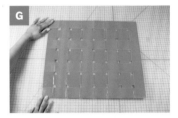

Pinch each corner into a triangle. Fold the point of the triangle down and inward along the bottom of the bag, making a perpendicular line at the 2" (5cm) mark. //I Hold the corners in place with small pieces of blue duct tape.//

12 To cover the seams, //J cut a 46" (117cm) strip of blue duct tape. Start at the top left edge of the bag and hold one end of the vertical strip. Place approximately 1" (2.5cm) of the strip above the top left edge and then press the rest of the strip down the left seam, across the bottom, and then up the right seam.//

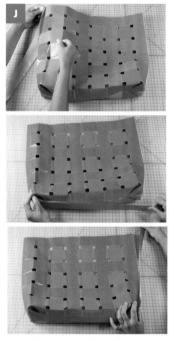

The other end of the strip should extend past the top edge of the right seam by approximately 1" (2.5cm). Fold the ends of the strip over the top edges on both the left and right seam.

13 TO MAKE THE STRAPS, cut 2 strips of 50" (127cm) orange duct tape and fold each one lengthwise into thirds.

14 //K On the front of the bag in the third column from the left edge, start at the top row and cut a 1" (2.5cm) horizontal slit in the center of the square formed by the intersecting column and row.//

//L Going down that column, cut 1" (2.5cm) wide slits in the center of the next 4 descending rows, lining them up directly below the first slit.//

15 Repeat step 14 on the right side of the front of the bag.

16 To attach one of the straps, //M start from the top and outside of the bag and weave one end of the strap through the slits on the left column.//

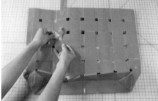

//N Weave the other end through the slits on the right column.//

Cover the strap ends on the inside of the bag vertically with 11" (28cm) strips of orange duct tape.

17 Repeat steps 14–16 on the back of the bag and attach the remaining strap from step 13.

LUNCH BAG

Surprise your friends at lunchtime with this fashion-forward take on a lunchbox. The sides of the bag are padded with linear pipe wrap—a bubble-wrap foil material that you can pick up at any hardware store—so it does keep food hot or cold for a few hours. Eating lunch has never looked so pretty!

DUCT TAPE
black (heavy duty), 8 yd (7.3m)
burgundy, 6 yd (5.5m)
white, 2 yd (1.8m)
pastel pink, 1 yd (0.9m)

ADDITIONAL MATERIALS
parchment paper, 10" × 9" (25.5cm × 23cm)
parchment paper, 10" × 3" (25.5cm × 7.5cm)
linear pipe wrap, 6" (15cm) wide, 3 yd (2.7m)
printout of template (see page 203),
    trimmed to outline of shape

TOOLS
• scissors
• craft knife
• metal ruler
• ballpoint pen
• white grease pencil

1 Place the larger parchment paper on the worktable in the portrait position. Make a duct tape fabric (see page 10) using 6 strips of 10" (25.5cm) black duct tape for the back side. Flip the working fabric over and place it in the landscape position so that the strips are vertical. Remove the parchment paper and set it aside. Cut a piece of linear pipe wrap that measures 9½" (24cm) long. Hold it in the landscape position over the back side of the duct tape fabric. **//A** Place the bottom edge of the pipe wrap approximately ¼" (6mm) above the bottom edge of the fabric and 1" (2.5cm) from the left and right edges.**//** Press the pipe wrap down.

2 **TO MAKE THE FRONT SIDE OF THE FIRST FABRIC,** **//B** cut 5 strips of 11" (28cm) burgundy duct tape and, starting at the bottom of the fabric, place them one above the other horizontally to cover the pipe wrap.**//**

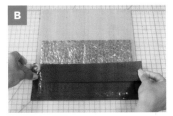

//C The long edge of each strip should overlap the strip placed previously by approximately ¼" (6mm), connecting them into one large piece.**//** Trim the fabric to 10" × 9" (25.5cm × 23cm) high.

3 Repeat steps 1 and 2 to make a second fabric. These are the front and back pieces of the bag.

4 **TO MAKE THE SIDES OF THE BAG,** make a third fabric using 5 strips of 8" (20.5cm) black duct tape for the back side and 4 strips of 7" (18cm) burgundy duct tape for the front side. Trim the fabric to 6" × 7" (15cm × 18cm). Cut it into 2 pieces that measure 3" × 7" (7.5cm × 18cm) each.

5 **TO MAKE THE BOTTOM OF THE BAG,** you will need to make a fourth fabric. Place the smaller parchment paper on the worktable in the portrait position and make the back side of the fabric using 6 strips of 4" (10cm) black duct tape.

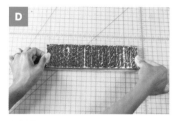

//D Flip it over and remove the parchment paper so the sticky side is facing up. Move the working fabric into the landscape position. Cut a piece of linear pipe wrap that measures 9½" × 2½" (24cm × 6.5cm). Place it in the center of the sticky side of the fourth fabric. **//E** Cut 2 strips of 11" (28cm) burgundy duct tape and place them one above the other in the horizontal position to cover the pipe wrap, the long edge of the second strip overlapping the first strip approximately ¼" (6mm).**//**

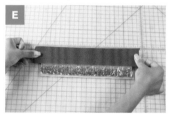

Trim the fabric to 10" × 3" (25.5cm × 7.5cm).

6 Place one of the main fabrics on the worktable in the landscape position, black duct tape side facing up, with the linear pipe wrap on its lower section. Place the bottom bag piece from step 5 in the landscape position below the

main fabric, the black duct tape side facing up, so the 10" (25.5cm) edges of the fabrics are touching and create a seam. **//F** Place a 10" (25.5cm) strip of black duct tape horizontally over the seam, connecting the 2 fabrics.**//**

7 Place the remaining main fabric in the landscape position on the worktable below the bottom bag piece, black side facing up, and the linear pipe wrap on its upper section, so that the 10" (25.5cm) edges of the fabrics are touching and create a seam. **//G** Place a 10" (25.5cm) strip of black duct tape horizontally over the seam, connecting the 2 fabrics.**//**

8 To attach the sides to the main bag, place one bag side each vertically along both the left and right edges of the bottom fabric, black duct tape sides facing up, lining up

the top edges with the seam between the bottom fabric and the bottom bag piece, and creating a seam between them. //**H** Place a 7" (18cm) strip of black duct tape vertically over each seam, attaching the sides to the bottom fabric.//

9 **TO MAKE THE MAIN POCKET OF THE BAG,** //**I** place a 3" (7.5cm) strip of black duct tape horizontally on the top edges of each bag side. Be sure that only half of the strip is attached to the fabric lengthwise.//

On the left bag side, fold back the tape strip on the top edge so the sticky half is facing up. Pull the left edge of the bottom

bag piece toward the top edge of the left bag side and press the tape strip down against the inside of the top fabric. Fold back the tape strip on the bottom edge of the left bag side so the sticky half is facing up. Pull the left edge of the top fabric toward the bottom edge of the left bag side and press the tape strip down against the inside of the bottom fabric. Repeat this step on the right bag side.

10 Place a 7" (18cm) strip of black duct tape vertically along the remaining long edge of the left bag side. Only half of the strip should be on the fabric lengthwise. Fold it back so the sticky half is facing up. //**J** Align the left edge of the bag side with the left edge of the top fabric. Press down the strip of tape, connecting the bag side to the fabric. Repeat this step on the right bag side. The main bag is now complete.//

11 Place the bag on the worktable with one of the main fabrics facing up and the opening at the top. //**K** Cut a strip of 21" (53.5cm) white duct tape and hold it horizontally. Line up the top edge of the white duct tape strip with the top edge of the bag and carefully place it on the bag.//

Fold the strip over the left and right edges of the bag and wrap it around the back side of the fabric.

12 **TO MAKE THE BAG HANDLES,** start at the top corners and measure 1" (2.5cm) down along the left and right edges and mark these points with a grease pencil. Draw a horizontal line connecting the 2 marks. Starting again from the top corners, measure 2" (5cm) down along the left and right edges and mark these points. Draw a horizontal line connecting these 2 marks. Starting from the left and right ends of the 1" (2.5cm) line, measure 2¼" (5.5cm) inward along the line and mark these points. Draw a vertical line at

(continued on next page)

each mark that ends at the horizontal line drawn at the 2" (5cm) mark. You should now have a rectangle that measures 5½" × 1" (14cm × 2.5cm). Using well-oiled scissors, cut out the rectangle from the fabric.

13 Flip the bag over and repeat steps 11 and 12.

14 **TO MAKE THE FLOWER,** place the larger parchment paper over the petal template and trace the petal 8 times in 2 rows of 4. Be sure the rows are as straight as possible. Place 2 strips of 18" (45.5cm) pastel pink duct tape on top of the parchment paper, covering the 2 rows of petal tracings. Flip the parchment paper over. You will still be able to see the tracings through the parchment paper.
//L Using a craft knife or well-oiled scissors, cut out the 8 petal stickers.**//**

15 Remove the parchment paper backing from the petal stickers. **//M** Draw a ¾" (2cm) diameter circle on the right-hand side of the front of the bag, 3" (7.5cm) from the top and right edges.**//**

//N Place the stickers on the bag and arrange them in 2 layers of 4 petals, the bases touching the circle.**//**

16 Place the smaller parchment paper over the template and trace the circle. Cover the circle with a 2" (5cm) strip of white regular duct tape, then flip the parchment paper

over. You will still be able to see the tracing. Cut out the circle sticker. **//O** Remove the parchment paper backing and place the circle sticker in the middle of the flower.**//**

17 To make the stem, cut a strip of white duct tape that measures ¼" wide × 4½" long (6mm × 11.5cm). **//P** Place it horizontally to the left of the flower on the front of the bag.**//**

SHOPPING SPREE

Take this tote to the mall and fill it with your purchases to avoid walking around with clunky boxes or cheapo bags that break before you get home. It doesn't look like a shopping bag, so no one needs to see what you've been buying, and if you purchase a surprise gift for a special person, you need not worry about roving eyes. Shopping Spree has your back.

DUCT TAPE

white (heavy duty), 14 yd
(12.8m)
tango chevron (Platypus brand),
11 yd (10m)
white oak (Platypus brand),
5 yd (4.6m)
green, 3 yd (2.7m)

ADDITIONAL MATERIALS

parchment paper, 18" × 15"
(45.5cm × 38cm)
grommet kit size #0, or ¼"
(6mm) diameter (*Note:* kit
should include inserting die,
hole cutter, inserting base,
wood block, and at least 4
pairs of brass grommets and
washers)

TOOLS

• scissors
• craft knife
• metal ruler
• white grease pencil
• hammer

1 For this project you will
need 2 fabrics. Place
the parchment paper on the
worktable in the landscape
position and make the first duct
tape fabric (see page 10) using
9 strips of 19" (48.5cm) white
duct tape for the back side and
11 strips of 16" (40.5cm) tango
chevron duct tape for the front
side. Trim the fabric to 18" ×
15" (45.5cm × 38cm).

2 **TO MAKE THE GREEN AND
WHITE-OAK STRIPED TOP
BORDER,** place the fabric from
step 1 on the worktable in the
landscape position with the
tango chevron side facing up.

From the top corners, measure
1" (2.5cm) down along the
left and right edges and mark.
Using a white grease pencil,
lightly draw a horizontal line
connecting the 2 marks. Cut
a 19" (48.5cm) strip of white-
oak duct tape and hold it
lengthwise, sticky side facing
down. **//A** Line up the bottom
edge of the strip with the 1"
(2.5cm) line on the fabric and
place it on the fabric.**//**
//B The top half of the white oak

duct tape strip will extend above
the top edge of the fabric;
fold it over to create a border at
the top of the fabric.**//** Trim the
excess tape at the left and right
sides.

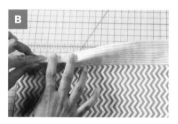

3 From the top corners,
measure 4½" (11.5cm)
down along the left and right
edges and mark with a grease
pencil. Lightly draw a horizontal
line connecting the 2 marks. To
make the green and white-oak

striped middle band, cut a 19"
(48.5cm) strip of white-oak duct
tape and trim off a lengthwise
strip 1" (2.5cm) wide. (Set
aside the extra tape, which will
be used in step 5.) Hold the 1"
(2.5cm) strip horizontally, sticky
side facing down. **//C** Line up
the bottom edge of the strip
with the 4½" (11.5cm) line and
place the strip on the fabric.**//**
Trim the excess tape at the left
and right sides.

4 Cut a 19" (48.5cm) strip of
green duct tape and trim off
2 strips lengthwise that are each
¾" (2cm) wide. Discard the
extra tape. **//D** Place a green
duct tape strip horizontally in
the center of the white-oak duct
tape border and the middle
band on the fabric.**//** Trim the
excess tape at the left and right
sides.

5 Cut the extra white-oak duct
tape strip from step 3 in
half lengthwise. **//E** Place one

of these strips horizontally in the center of the green strip on the top border and the middle band.// Trim the excess tape at the left and right sides.

6 Repeat steps 1–5 to make the second fabric.

7 Place one duct tape fabric above the other on the worktable in the landscape position, the tango chevron sides facing up and two 18" (45.5cm) sides adjacent. The white-oak and green stripe border should be on the top edge for the upper fabric and the bottom edge for the other fabric. Flip the fabrics over from left to right, maintaining the orientation of the borders as described. The white duct tape sides are now facing up. Line up the fabrics so the 18" (45.5cm) edges touch and create a middle seam. //F Place an 18" (45.5cm) strip of white duct tape horizontally over the seam, connecting the 2 fabrics.//

8 Place a strip of 15" (38cm) white duct tape vertically on the left and right edges of the fabric at the top. Be sure that only half of the strips are on the fabric lengthwise. //G On the left edge, fold back the tape strip so the sticky half is facing up. Pull up the fabric at the bottom and fold it horizontally at the middle seam. It should completely cover the first fabric. Line up the left edges and press down the folded tape strip to secure the seams. Repeat on the right edge.//

9 To flatten the bottom of the bag, //H measure 2" (5cm) inward from each corner along the bottom edge and mark with a grease pencil. Pinch each corner into a triangle. Fold the point of the triangle down and inward along the bottom of the bag, making a perpendicular line at the 2" (5cm) mark. Hold the corners in place with small pieces of white duct tape.//

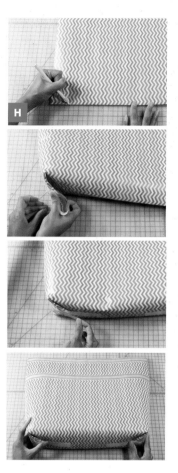

10 To cover the side seams, cut a 17" (43cm) strip of white-oak duct tape and trim off 2 strips lengthwise that are each ½" (13mm) wide. Discard the rest of the tape. Starting at the top left edge of the bag and holding one end of the strip vertically, place approximately 2" (5cm) of the strip above the top edge and then press the rest of the strip down the left seam, across the bottom, and then up

(continued on next page)

the right seam. The other end of the strip should extend past the top edge of the right seam by approximately 2" (5cm). Fold the ends of the strip over the top edges on both the left and right seam.

11 //I Place a strip of 13" (33cm) white-oak duct tape lengthwise across the bottom of the bag, from bottom corner to bottom corner.//

12 TO MAKE THE STRAPS, place a 33" (84cm) strip of white duct tape on the worktable, sticky side facing down. //J Place a 33" (84cm) strip of white-oak duct tape on top of it, sticky side facing down. The second strip should line up with the edges of the first strip, completely covering it. The strip you've made is now 2-ply.//

Flip this strip over so the sticky side is facing up. Cut a 27" (68.5cm) strip of green duct tape and hold it with the sticky side facing down. Before placing the green duct tape strip down, carefully line up the long edges of the green duct tape strip with the 2-ply strip as much as possible and center the green tape so that there are approximately 3" (7.5cm) of the sticky side exposed at each short end. //K After placing the green duct tape strip on the 2-ply strip, trim off 2 strips lengthwise that have a width of ¼" (6mm) each. Discard the rest of the tape.//

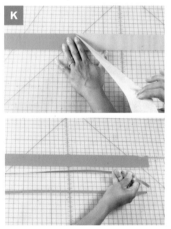

13 From the top left corner of the bag, measure 3" (7.5cm) inward along the top edge and mark with a grease pencil. Starting from this point,

measure 1½" (3.8cm) straight down and mark this point. Repeat from the top right corner of the bag.

//L Following the directions on the grommet kit, insert a grommet at each of these 2 points.//

14 Starting from the outside of the bag, push approximately 4" (10cm) of one end of the strap through the left grommet. Repeat with the other end of the strap and the right grommet. Fold over the end of each strap so the exposed sticky section adheres to the back side of the strap.

15 Repeat steps 13 and 14 on the other side of the bag using the remaining strap. Cut a 6" (15cm) strip of green duct tape and trim off 4 strips lengthwise that measure ¼" (6mm) wide each. Vertically place a strip on the back of each strap where the end folds over. Discard the rest of the green tape strip.

ALONG THE DIAGONAL

With its bright orange frame and zigzagging lines, this bag is meant for the stylish gal about town. Complementing the diagonal pleats, a roomy outside pocket holds car keys or the lip gloss that perpetually gets lost at the bottom of a bag.

DUCT TAPE
white (heavy duty), 17 yd
    (15.5m)
tango linen (Platypus brand),
    7 yd (6.4m)
pool chevron (Platypus brand),
    11 yd (10m)

ADDITIONAL MATERIALS
parchment paper, 15" × 13"
    (38cm × 33cm)
4 O-rings, 1½" (3.8cm) diameter

TOOLS
• scissors
• craft knife
• metal ruler
• graphite pencil
• white grease pencil

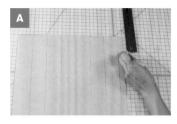

3 **//B** Cut a 5½" (14cm) strip of tango linen duct tape and hold it diagonally above the top right corner of the fabric, sticky side facing down.**//**

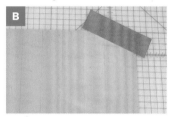

Line up the bottom edge of the strip with the marks made in step 2, creating a diagonal line. Place the strip on the fabric.

4 Cut one 9½" (24cm), one 13½" (34.5cm), and one 16½" (42cm) strip of tango linen duct tape and place them on the worktable with the sticky sides facing up. On each strip, fold back one long edge approximately ⅛" (3mm) to create pleated strips. Flip each strip over and, starting with the shortest strip and proceeding to the longest, place them onto the fabric diagonally beneath the first strip from step 3. The folded long edge of each pleated strip should face up along the top. Each strip should barely overlap the strip before it.

//NOTE: Platypus tape is thicker than other brands of duct tape. Folds in the duct tape will eventually unfold, so be sure the pleats are not overlapping the previous strip of tape by more than ¹⁄₁₆" (1.5mm). This will ensure that the fold on the back side of each pleated strip will adhere to the sticky back side of the working fabric.**//**

5 Cut 7 strips of 16" (40.5cm) pool chevron duct tape and place them on the worktable with the sticky sides facing up. On each strip, fold back one long edge approximately ⅛" (3mm) to create pleated strips. **//C** Flip each strip over and place them onto the fabric diagonally beneath the tango linen pleats. The folded long edges of each pleated strip should face up. Each strip should barely overlap the one before it.**//**

6 Flip the fabric over so the white side is facing up and trim the fabric to 13" × 15" (33cm × 38cm). Set aside.

7 Repeat steps 1–6 to make the second fabric.

1 For this project, you will need 3 fabrics. Place the parchment paper on the worktable in the landscape position and make the first duct tape fabric (see page 10) using 8 strips of 16" (40.5cm) white duct tape for the back side. After completing the back side, flip the working fabric over so the parchment paper is facing up. Trim the fabric to 13" × 15" (33cm × 38cm). Gently peel off the parchment paper, exposing the sticky side of the fabric. Be sure the fabric is now in the portrait position. Set aside the parchment paper.

2 **//A** Starting at the top right corner of the working fabric, measure 4" (10cm) inward along the top edge and mark with a grease pencil. Starting again at the top right corner, measure 2" (5cm) down along the right edge and mark.**//**

8 Place one duct tape fabric above the other on the worktable in the portrait position with the pleated sides facing up. The fabric at the top should have the tango linen triangle section at the upper right corner, and the bottom fabric should have it at the lower left corner. Flip both fabrics over left to right (maintaining the orientation of the tango linen triangle) so that the white duct tape side is facing up and the edges are touching and creating a middle seam. **//D** Connect the fabrics by placing a strip of 13" (33cm) white duct tape horizontally over the seam.**//**

9 Place a strip of 15" (38cm) white duct tape vertically on both the left and right edges of the top fabric. Be sure that only half of the strips are on the fabric lengthwise. **//E** On the left edge, fold back the tape strip so the sticky half is facing up.**//**

//F Pull up the bottom fabric and fold it horizontally at the middle seam. It should completely cover the other fabric.**//**

Line up the left edges and press down the folded tape strip to secure the seams. Repeat this step on the right edge.

10 **TO MAKE THE THIRD FABRIC FOR THE POCKET,** place the parchment paper on the worktable in the landscape position. Make the back side of the fabric using 8 strips of 16" (40.5cm) white duct tape. Flip the working fabric over so the parchment paper is facing up. Trim the fabric to 13" × 15" (33cm × 38cm).

11 With this fabric in the portrait position and the parchment paper side facing up and starting from the bottom left corner, measure 8½" (21.5cm) up along the left edge and mark with a grease pencil. Align the metal ruler diagonally with the 8½" (21.5cm) mark on the left edge and the top right corner. **//G** Cut the fabric with a well-oiled craft knife by pushing the blade down against the ruler. Discard the top portion of the fabric.**//** Remove the parchment paper to expose the sticky side.

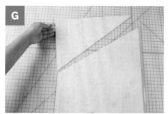

12 Cut 7 strips of 15½" (39.5cm) pool chevron duct tape and one strip of 15½" (39.5cm) tango linen duct tape and place them on the worktable with the sticky sides facing up. On each strip, fold back one long edge approximately ⅛" (3mm) to create pleated strips.

13 Flip one of the pleated pool chevron strips over and hold it so the folded edge is at the top. Place the fabric from step 10 in front of you on the worktable and line up the top long edge of the pool chevron strip with the diagonal top edge of the fabric where you cut it and carefully place the chevron strip down. **//H** Place the remaining pleated pool chevron strips, sticky side facing down and folded edge at the top, onto the fabric diagonally beneath the first pleated strip.**//**

(continued on next page)

Each strip should barely overlap the strip before it. Hold the tango pleated strip so the folded edge is on the bottom. Place it over the top edge of the fabric diagonally so that only half of the strip is on the fabric lengthwise. Fold the extra strip over the top edge. Flip the fabric over and trim the pleated strips extending over the sides to match the edges of the white duct tape side. //I This is the pocket fabric.//

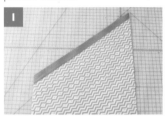

14 Flip the pocket fabric over so the white duct tape side is facing up. Be sure that the diagonal edge is still at the top. Place the pocket fabric on the right side of the connected fabrics from step 8. The top left corner of the pocket fabric should line up with the top right corner of the main fabric so the sides touch and create a seam. //J Place a 15" (38cm) strip of white duct tape vertically over the seam.//

Place an 8½" (21.5cm) strip of white duct tape vertically on the right edge of the pocket fabric, so that only half of the strip is on the fabric lengthwise. Fold back the tape strip so the sticky half faces up, then pull the pocket fabric to the left so that the left edge of the pocket fabric aligns with the left edge of the main fabric below it. //K Press down along the left edge of both fabrics so the folded tape strip connects them.//

15 To flatten the bottom of the bag, //L measure 2" (5cm) inward from each bottom corner along the bottom edge and mark with a grease pencil.//

Pinch each corner into a triangle. Fold the point of the triangle down and inward along the bottom of the bag, making a perpendicular line at the 2" (5cm) mark. //M Hold the corners in place with small pieces of white duct tape.//

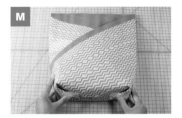

16 To cover the seams, cut a 38" (96.5cm) strip of tango linen duct tape. //N Starting at the top left edge of the bag and holding one end of the vertical strip, place approximately 2" (5cm) of the strip above the top edge and then press the rest of the strip down the left seam, across the bottom, and then up the right seam.//

The other end of the strip should extend past the top edge of the right seam by approximately 2" (5cm). Fold the ends of the strip over the top of both seams.

17 TO MAKE A STRAP, cut a 36" (91cm) strip of white duct tape and a 36"

(91cm) strip of tango linen duct tape. Stick them together. Cut the width down to 1" (2.5cm). Repeat to make the second strap. From each strap, cut off a 10" (25.5cm) piece. Set aside the longer pieces, which are the main straps.

18 Cut the 2 remaining 10" (25.5cm) pieces in half so there are a total of 4 pieces that measure 5" (12.5cm) each. Fold one of these 5" (12.5cm) pieces in half crosswise and rotate it so the folded end is at the bottom. Starting at the right bottom corner, measure ¼" (6mm) inward along the folded edge and mark it. Starting again at the right bottom corner, measure 1" (2.5cm) up the right edge and mark it. //O Cut off the right corner using these marks. Repeat this step on the left side to cut off the left corner.//

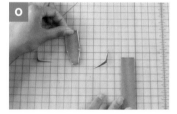

This is the strap loop that will attach to an O-ring. When unfolded, the strap loop has an hourglass shape.

19 Repeat step 18 with the other three 5" (12.5cm) pieces. There should be a total of 4 strap loops. Set them aside.

20 Place one of the main straps lengthwise on the worktable, white duct tape side facing up. //P Fold one short end of the strap in approximately 2" (5cm). Repeat step 18 on this folded end so when it is unfolded it has an hourglass shape.// Then repeat this step on the remaining strap.

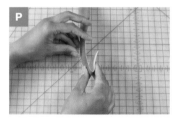

21 Place the O-rings on the worktable. Refold the hourglass-shaped ends of each main strap through an O-ring and secure it on the back side of the strap with 1" (2.5cm) strips of white duct tape. Place the strap loops from steps 18 and 19 on the worktable. //Q On the opposite side of each O-ring, refold the hourglass-shaped end of a strap loop. Wrap a 1" (2.5cm) strip of white duct tape around each wide bottom of the strap loop to keep it closed.//

22 You will now attach the straps to the bag. From the top corners of the bag, measure 1" (2.5cm) down along the left and right edges and mark these points with a grease pencil. Draw a horizontal line across the bag connecting the 2 marks. Starting at the left end of the drawn line, measure 3½" (9cm) in and mark this point. From this point and cutting to the right, make a ¾" (2cm) horizontal slit. Starting at the right end of the drawn line, measure 3½" (9cm) inward and mark this point. From this point and cutting to the left, make a ¾" (2cm) horizontal slit.

23 //R Insert the strap-loop ends of a bag strap into the slits. You will need to vertically fold each strap piece to fit through the slits.// To secure the straps to the bag, place a 4½" (11.5cm) strip of white duct tape vertically over each strap piece on the inside of the bag.

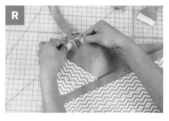

24 Repeat steps 22 and 23 to attach the remaining strap to the back of the bag.

PERSONALIZED TOTE

This bag is roomy enough for a last-minute camping trip as well as a visit to a big-box store. But who says that you need to sacrifice fashion for function? This personalized tote does it all. And don't worry about getting the bag dirty—because duct tape is waterproof, you can always give it a rinse before storing it.

DUCT TAPE
black (heavy duty), 15 yd (13.7m)
teal, 11 yd (10m)
white, 3 yd (2.7m)
black (regular), 4 yd (3.7m)

ADDITIONAL MATERIALS
parchment paper, 18" × 15"
    (45.5cm × 38cm)
printout of template (see page 200),
    trimmed to outline of shape

TOOLS
• scissors
• craft knife
• metal ruler
• graphite pencil
• white grease pencil

1 For this project you will need 2 fabrics. Place the parchment paper on the worktable in the portrait position and make the first duct tape fabric (see page 10) using 11 strips of 16" (40.5cm) black heavy-duty duct tape for the back side and 9 strips of 19" (48.5cm) teal duct tape for the front side. Trim the fabric to 18" × 15" (45.5cm × 38cm). Repeat this step to make the second fabric. Set aside the parchment paper. (You will use it in step 5.)

2 Place one duct tape fabric above the other on the worktable in the landscape position, the black heavy-duty duct tape side facing up, with two 18" (45.5cm) edges touching and creating a middle seam. **//A** Place an 18" (45.5cm) strip of black heavy-duty duct tape horizontally over the seam, connecting the 2 fabrics.**//**

3 //B Place a strip of 15" (38cm) black heavy-duty duct tape vertically on both of the left and right edges of the fabric at the top. Be sure that only half of the strips are on the fabric lengthwise. On the left edge, fold back the tape strip so the sticky half is facing up. Pull up the bottom fabric and fold it at the middle seam.// It should completely cover the first fabric. Line up the left edges and press down the folded tape strip to secure the seams. Repeat on the right edge.

TIPS To make sure your chosen word or phrase fits evenly inside the panel, count out the number of letters. If it's a phrase, be sure to add the space or spaces in between the words to your number. Then divide 18 by that number. The result is the approximate width of each letter/space, give or take ¼" (6mm).

Before drawing the block letters, mark off the vertical center of the panel. Also determine which letter is in the middle of the word or phrase. If the number of letters/spaces is an odd number, then the middle letter or space will be directly in the center of the panel. If it is an even number, then there will be a letter or space on each side of the vertical center mark.

To cut the letters out cleanly, be sure to oil your scissors or craft knife after cutting out each letter.

4 To flatten the bottom of the bag, measure 2" (5cm) inward from the corners along the bottom edge and mark with a grease pencil. Pinch each corner into a triangle. Fold the point of the triangle down and inward along the bottom of the bag, making a perpendicular line at the 2" (5cm) mark. Hold the corners in place with small pieces of black heavy-duty duct tape. Place a strip of 13" (33cm) teal duct tape lengthwise across the bottom of the bag, from bottom corner to bottom corner.

5 **TO MAKE THE FRONT PANEL,** place the left side of the parchment paper over the template. Use a graphite pencil

to trace the outline of the panel. Note that this is only half of the panel. Flip the parchment paper over from left to right so that the left side of the parchment paper is blank. Place the parchment paper over the template again and line up the wider end of the tracing with the wider end of the panel template. Trace the other side of the panel. Place 4 strips of 19" (48.5cm) white duct tape horizontally over the panel tracing. Be sure the long edge of each strip overlaps the previously placed strip approximately ¼" (6mm), connecting them into one piece. Flip the strips and the parchment paper over so you can see the tracing. //C Using a craft knife, cut out the panel sticker.//

6 Peel off the parchment-paper backing from the panel sticker. Set aside the parchment paper. //D Center the sticker horizontally on one side of the bag.//

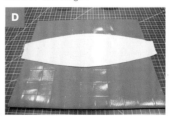

7 **TO MAKE THE PERSONALIZED STICKERS,**
//E use a graphite pencil and draw block letters on the parchment paper from step 6. Note that they must be block or bubble letters in order to make stickers. You can spell out your name or monogram (see Tip at left).//

Place 4 strips of 19" (48.5cm) black regular duct tape horizontally over the letters. Be sure the long edge of each strip overlaps the previously placed strip approximately ¼" (6mm), connecting them into one piece. Flip the strips and the parchment paper over so you can see the letters. //F Using a craft knife, cut out the outline of the letters. Discard the extra tape and parchment paper.//

8 Arrange the letter stickers on the white duct tape panel so they are equally spaced. When you are satisfied with the placement of the letter stickers, peel off the parchment-paper backing from the letter stickers one by one and place them on top of the white duct tape panel.

9 **TO MAKE THE STRAPS,** cut a 29" (74cm) strip of black heavy-duty duct tape and a 29" (74cm) strip of black regular duct tape. Stick them together. Cut 2 lengthwise strips, each with a width of ½" (13mm). Discard the rest of the tape.

10 From the top left corner of the front of the bag, measure 4½" (11.5cm) inward along the top edge and mark this point with a grease pencil. From there, measure 1½" (3.8cm) straight down and mark it. From there and moving toward the right, cut a ¾" (2cm) wide horizontal slit into the fabric. Starting at the top right corner of the front of the bag, repeat this step to make a second slit.

11 Starting from the front of the bag, push approximately 4" (10cm) of the end of one of the straps through the left slit. Repeat with the other end of the strap and the right slit. To prevent the straps from puckering around the slit, angle the straps toward the middle. Place a 6" (15cm) strip of black heavy-duty duct tape vertically over each strap end on the inside of the bag.

12 Repeat steps 10 and 11 on the back of the bag to attach the remaining strap.

SLING, BOWLER & HANDBAG

These seven bags all defy the conventional wisdom that duct tape fabric lacks the ability to be supple. Duct tape can indeed be shaped into an interesting silhouette, a loosely woven cylinder, a disco ball, an assemblage of overlapping straps, a whimsical birdie, a bouquet of flowers, and a wood-veneer jigsaw puzzle. Duct tape is not just duct tape; duct tape is a raw material. And we should use it to create not just bags but the unexpected.

DUCT TAPE
black (heavy duty), 18 yd (16.4m)
dark blue, 4 yd (3.7m)
orange, 2 yd (1.8m)
black (regular), 8 yd (7.3m)

ADDITIONAL MATERIALS
parchment paper, 27" × 9½"
    (68.5cm × 24cm)
parchment paper, 8" × 8"
    (20.5cm × 20.5cm)
printout of template (see page
    201), trimmed to outline of
    shape
metal slider, 2" (5cm)

TOOLS
• scissors
• craft knife
• metal ruler
• white grease pencil

1 For this project, you will need 3 fabrics. Place the larger parchment paper on the worktable in the landscape position and begin making the first duct tape fabric (see page 10) using 6 strips of 28" (71cm) black heavy-duty duct tape for the back side. **//A** Flip it over and place it on the worktable. Remove the parchment paper and set it aside.**//** (You will use it again in step 6.)

2 **TO MAKE THE FRONT SIDE,** you will attach the strips vertically. **//B** Starting on the right edge and working toward the left, place 11 strips of 10½" (26.5cm) dark blue duct tape. Add 5 strips of 10½" (26.5cm) orange duct tape.**//**

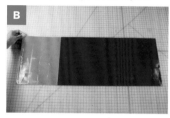

Be sure the strips overlap at the long ends by approximately ⅛" (3mm). Trim the fabric to 27" × 9½" (68.5cm × 24cm) high.

3 From the top and bottom left corners of the front fabric, measure inward 13½" (34.5cm) along the top and bottom edges and mark these points with a grease pencil. Draw a vertical line connecting the 2 marks. **//C** From the top of the drawn line, measure downward 1¾" (4.5cm) and mark this point.**//**

//D From the bottom of the drawn line, measure up 1¾" (4.5cm) and mark it.**//** Cut a 6" (15cm) vertical slit on the line between the 2 marks.

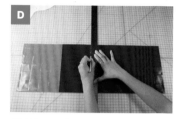

//E Cover the slit vertically with an 8" × 1" (20.5cm × 2.5cm) strip of black regular duct tape, then recut the 6" (15cm) slit again.**//**

This is the opening of the pocket, which you will make next.

4 **//F** Place the smaller parchment paper on the worktable and make a second duct tape fabric using 5 strips of 9" (23cm) black heavy-duty tape for the back side and 5 strips of 9" (23cm) black regular tape for the front side.**//**

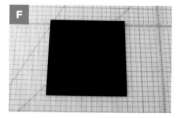

Trim the fabric down to 8" × 8" (20.5cm × 20.5cm). This is the pocket fabric.

5 Place the front fabric on the worktable with the black heavy-duty duct tape side facing up. //G Place the pocket fabric on the front fabric so it's centered over the slit.

//H Place 10" (25.5cm) strips of black heavy-duty duct tape over each edge of the pocket fabric so that it is attached to the front fabric.//

6 MAKE A THIRD DUCT TAPE FABRIC FOR THE BACK OF THE BAG using the larger parchment paper from step 1, 6 strips of 28" (71cm) black heavy-duty duct tape for the back side, and 16 strips of 10½" (26.5cm) black regular duct tape for the front side. Trim the fabric to 27" × 9½" (68.5cm × 24cm) high.

7 Place the front fabric on the worktable in the landscape position, black heavy-duty duct tape side facing up. //I Hold the template in the landscape position with the bottleneck-shaped end facing left. Place it on the left half of the fabric, lining up the left, top, and bottom edges of the template as much as possible with the fabric edges. Trace the outline onto the fabric with a grease pencil. Flip the template from left to right so the bottleneck shape is facing right. Place it on the right half of the fabric, lining up the right, top, and bottom edges of the template as much as possible with the fabric's edges. Trace the outline onto the fabric. Remove the template and cut the fabric along the template outlines using a pair of well-oiled scissors.//

8 //J Repeat step 7 on the back fabric.//

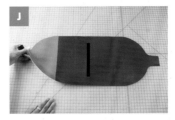

9 TO MAKE A BAG SIDE, //K cut a 28" (71cm) strip of black heavy-duty duct tape and a 28" (71cm) strip of black regular duct tape.// Stick them together. Repeat this step to make the other bag side.

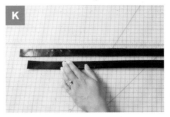

10 Place one of the bag sides on the worktable in the landscape position, black heavy-duty duct tape side facing up. Attach a 28" (71cm) strip of black heavy-duty duct tape lengthwise along both the top and bottom long edges. Be sure only half of the strip is on the fabric lengthwise. Turn the fabric over so that the sticky half of each strip is facing up.

(continued on next page)

11 Place the front fabric on the worktable in the landscape position below the bag side, the blue-and-orange side facing up. //L Starting on the left end of both the bag side and front fabric, attach the bag side to the front fabric by aligning the edges and pressing the exposed tape strip against the back side of the front fabric.//

12 //M Place the back fabric on the worktable in the landscape position above the bag side, the black regular duct tape side facing up. Starting on the left end of both the bag side and back fabric, attach the bag side to the back fabric by aligning the edges and pressing the exposed tape strip against the back side of the back fabric.//

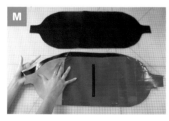

Turn the connected fabrics so the unattached long edges of the front and back fabrics are on the bottom.

13 Repeat step 10. Place the bag side on the worktable in the landscape position below the front and back fabrics, black regular duct tape side facing up. //N Attach the top edge of the second bag side to the bottom edge of the front fabric, aligning the edges and pressing the exposed tape strip against the back side of the front fabric.//

//O Attach the bottom edge of the second bag side to the bottom edge of the back fabric, aligning the edges and pressing the exposed tape strip against the back side of the back fabric. The main pocket of the bag is complete.//

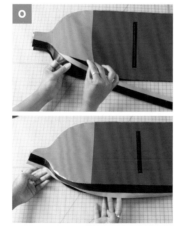

14 TO MAKE THE BAG OPENING, place the bag on the worktable in the portrait position with the front side facing up and the orange section at the top. Flip the bag from left to right. //P Approximately 7" (18cm) from the top edge, cut a 7½" (19cm) horizontal slit on the back of the bag only.// Do NOT cut through to the front of the bag.

15 TO MAKE A STRAP, cut a 25" (63.5cm) strip of black heavy-duty duct tape and a 25" (63.5cm) strip of black regular duct tape. Stick them together. Repeat this step for the second strap.

16 **//Q** Place an end of one strap approximately 2" (5cm) into the opening at the top of the bag.**//**

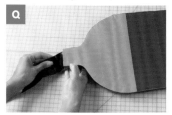

//R Cut 3" (7.5cm) strips of black heavy-duty duct tape and place them vertically inside the bag opening to cover the end of the bag strap, attaching it to the inside of the bag.**//**

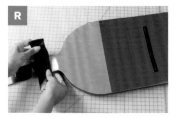

//S Horizontally wrap a 6" (15cm) strip of black heavy-duty duct tape around the bag opening, covering the edges.**//**

Turn the bag over so the remaining bag opening is on the top. Repeat this step with the other bag strap.

17 **//T** Cut a strip of 10½" (26.5cm) black regular duct tape and trim it down lengthwise to 1" (2.5cm) wide. Discard any excess black tape.

Place the black strip vertically over the border between the dark blue and orange duct tape strips.**//**

18 Loop a metal slider through the unattached end of the second strap, leaving a 1" (2.5cm) tail. Fold the tail over the middle bar of the slider and secure it with a 1" (2.5cm) strip of black heavy-duty duct tape. Weave the open end of the first strap through the slider.

PULL STRING SLING

With its cylindrical shape and loosely woven framework, this bag can carry Frisbees, volleyballs, or a few dozen baseballs to the park. Or it can hold a pair of muddy sneakers after a day of trail running. And unlike the ever-present sports brand pull string bags, this one lets its contents breathe.

DUCT TAPE
yellow, 9 yd (8.2m)
black (heavy duty), 10 yd (9.1m)
black-and-white graphic swirl, 7 yd (6.4m)

ADDITIONAL MATERIALS
2 pieces of parchment paper, each
    measuring 8" × 8" (20.5cm × 20.5cm)

TOOLS
• scissors
• craft knife
• metal ruler
• protractor
• white grease pencil

1 Cut 16 strips of 17" (43cm) yellow duct tape. Fold each strip in half lengthwise. Arrange them on the worktable vertically approximately ½" (13mm) apart. Place small strips of black duct tape at the top and bottom ends of each strip so they don't move on the worktable.

2 Cut 9 strips of 24" (61cm) black-and-white graphic-swirl duct tape. Fold each strip in half lengthwise.

//A Starting approximately ½" (13mm) from the top edges of the yellow tape strips on the worktable, weave the graphic-swirl strips through the yellow strips in rows that are approximately ½" (13mm) apart from each other.**//**

3 Cut 3 strips of 25" (63.5cm) black duct tape and cut each one in half lengthwise. Cut each strip in half lengthwise again. You should have 12 strips that are each approximately ½" (13mm) wide. Place one strip horizontally across the middle of each graphic-swirl row. Discard the extra black duct tape strips.

4 Cut 4 strips of 17" (43cm) black duct tape and cut each one in half lengthwise. Cut each strip in half lengthwise again. You should have 16 strips

that are each approximately ½" (13mm) wide. //B Place a black strip vertically down the middle of each yellow column.//
The back side of the fabric is now complete.

5 Remove the small strips of black duct tape from step 1 that were holding down the top and bottom edges of the yellow duct tape columns. Trim the top edges of each yellow duct tape column evenly, approximately ½" (13mm) from the top of the first graphic-swirl row. //C On each yellow duct tape column, measure 1" (2.5cm) down from the bottom of the last graphic-swirl row and mark the point with a grease pencil.//

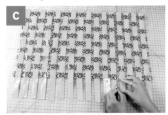

6 With the back side of the fabric still facing up from the worktable, bring the left and right ends of the top graphic-swirl row together. //D Wrap a ½" (13mm) strip of graphic-swirl duct tape vertically around the ends to connect each row to itself.

Repeat this on the other 8 rows.//

7 TO MAKE THE PULL STRING LOOPS, cut 9 strips of 2" (5cm) black duct tape and place them on the worktable with the sticky sides facing up. Cut 9 strips of 1" (2.5cm) black duct tape and horizontally place each one, sticky side facing down, in the horizontal center of a 2" (5cm) strip; ½" (13mm) of the sticky part will remain exposed on either the top or bottom edges. Cut each set in half vertically. There should now be 18 double-sided strips with partial sticky sides.

8 Hold one of these strips in the portrait position with the partial sticky side facing up. The bottom edge should have a ½" (13mm) wide section of exposed sticky side. //E Line up the bottom edge of the strip with the top edge of the first graphic-swirl duct tape row of the main bag and place the strip down on the yellow duct tape

column from the back side. Part of the strip will extend over the top edge of the bag.//

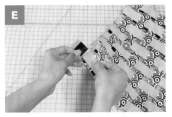

Fold the strip horizontally in half over the top of the yellow duct tape column, creating a loop on top. Repeat to cover the remaining yellow duct tape columns. There should be 2 pull string loops left. Set one aside and discard the other. //F Along the top edge, cut a ¼" × ¼" (6mm × 6mm) V shape into the center of the folded edge of each pull string loop attached to the woven fabric.//

9 TO MAKE THE BACK SIDE OF THE BOTTOM OF THE BAG, place one of the parchment paper squares on the worktable and make one side of a duct tape fabric (see page 10) using 5 strips of 9" (23cm) black duct tape. //G Use the protractor and draw a circle with an 8" (20.5cm) diameter in the center of the fabric.// Cut out the circle with a pair of well-oiled scissors. The

parchment paper should still be on the back of the bag bottom. On the black duct tape side measure and mark every 1½" (3.8cm) around the perimeter using a grease pencil.

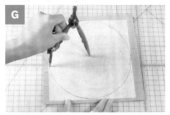

10 You will now attach the ends of each yellow duct tape column to the perimeter of the bag bottom. Hold the main body of the bag upside down so the pull string loops are at the bottom. Hold the bag bottom so that it is inside the main body of the bag and the parchment-paper side is facing up. Partially pull back the parchment paper from the bag bottom, exposing approximately half of the sticky side. **// H** Horizontally fold 8 of the yellow duct-tape columns over the sticky side of the bag bottom at each 1½" (3.8cm) mark.**//**

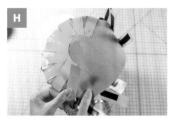

Pull off the rest of the parchment paper and horizontally fold the remaining 8 ends of the yellow duct-tape columns over the sticky side of the bag bottom at each 1½" (3.8cm) mark.

11 **TO MAKE THE FRONT SIDE OF THE BAG BOTTOM,** repeat step 9 using the second piece of parchment paper. Set aside.

12 Place the remaining pull string loop from step 8 in the portrait position with the partial sticky side facing down. **//I** Place one sticky end on the perimeter of the circle sticker between 2 of the yellow duct tape columns. Fold the strip in half so the remaining sticky end is facing up.**//**

Partially pull back the parchment paper from the front side of the bag bottom, exposing approximately half of the sticky side. Carefully place it on top of the back side of the bag bottom, over the folded pull string loop. Be sure to line up the edges of the front and back side of the bag bottom. **//J** Pull the rest of the parchment paper off the front bag bottom and stick the rest of it to the back side of the bag bottom.**//**

13 **TO MAKE THE PULL STRING,** cut a 40" (101.5cm) strip of black duct tape. Fold it in half lengthwise. Trim off 2 strips lengthwise, each with a width of ¼" (6mm). Discard the rest of the tape. Bring one end of each strip together and wrap a 2" (5cm) strip of black duct tape around them, forming an 80" (203cm) pull string. **//K** Push one end of the pull string through the 16 pull string loops on the top of the bag. Pull the same end of the pull string through the sixteenth loop until the tail is approximately 2" (5cm) longer than the other end of the pull string. Push that same end of the pull string through the bottom pull string loop.**//**

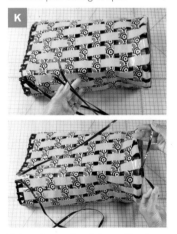

Bring the ends of the pull string together. Wrap a 2" (5cm) strip of black duct tape around them, forming a loop.

FLOWER GIRL

If you were ever lucky enough to be a flower girl, then this blossomy bowler may bring back memories of rose petal baskets and daisy crowns. It also proves that duct tape flowers can be delicate, and that any print or pattern can make a pretty flower. Instead of an organza gown, a casual sundress would be the perfect partner. No matter the dress, a stroll through the park—shoes optional!—with the Flower Girl in hand can make you feel like a princess.

DUCT TAPE
white (heavy duty), 7 yd (6.4m)
purple, 2 yd (1.8m)
Blue Plate (Scotch brand), 25 yd (22.8m)

ADDITIONAL MATERIALS
parchment paper, 8" × 12"
   (20.5cm × 30.5cm)

TOOLS
• scissors
• craft knife
• metal ruler
• graphite pencil
• ballpoint pen (any color)
• white grease pencil
• circles inking template
• awl

1 Place the parchment paper on the worktable in the landscape position and make a duct tape fabric (see page 10) using 5 strips of 13" (33cm) white duct tape for the back side and 7 strips of 9" (23cm) purple duct tape for the front side. Trim the fabric to 8" × 12" (20.5cm × 30.5cm). Set aside the parchment paper. (You will use it again in step 4.)

2 Set the fabric on the worktable in the portrait position, white side facing up. Place a strip of 6" (15cm) white duct tape vertically on both the left and right edges of the top fabric. Be sure that only half of each strip is on the fabric lengthwise. //A On the left edge, fold back the tape strip so the sticky half is facing up. Pull up the bottom of the fabric and fold it in half horizontally at the middle seam.// Line up

the left edges and press down the folded tape strip to secure the seams. Repeat on the right edge.

3 To flatten the bottom of the bag, measure 2" (5cm)

inward along the bottom edge from both corners and mark with a grease pencil. //B Pinch each corner into a triangle. Fold the point of the triangle down and inward along the bottom of the bag, making a perpendicular line at the 2" (5cm) mark. Hold the corners in place with small pieces of white heavy-duty duct tape.//

//C Place a strip of 4" (10cm) purple duct tape lengthwise across the bottom of the bag, from bottom corner to bottom corner.//

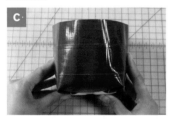

4 **TO MAKE THE CIRCLE STICKERS,** place the parchment paper on the table. Using the circles inking template and a graphite pencil, draw 4 straight rows of 4 circles, each with a diameter of 1⅝" (4cm). Cover each row with a strip of 10" (25.5cm) white duct tape. Flip over the parchment paper. You should be able to see the circles

through the parchment paper. //D With a pair of well-oiled scissors, cut out each circle.//

You should have 16 circle stickers. Discard the excess paper and tape. //E In the center of every circle sticker, use a ballpoint pen and circles inking template to draw a smaller circle with a diameter of 1¹/₁₆" (2.7cm).//

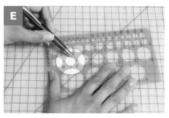

5 Cut 2 strips of 26" (66cm) Blue Plate duct tape. Stick them together. You now have a double-sided strip. //F Cut the strip into 3 pieces: 12" (30.5cm), 8" (20.5cm), and 6" (15cm).//

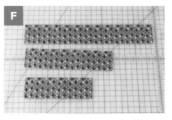

6 Cut a strip of 5½" (14cm) white duct tape in half

lengthwise. Set aside one of the strips for step 7. Cut the other strip into 2 pieces: 3½" (9cm) and 2" (5cm). Place them on the worktable with the sticky side facing up.

7 **YOU WILL NOW MAKE A FLOWER. FOR THE LARGE-SIZE RUFFLES,** place the 5½" (14cm) strip of white duct tape from step 6 on the worktable in the vertical position, sticky side facing up. //G Attach one of the long ends of the 12" (30.5cm) double-sided strip of Blue Plate duct tape to half the length of the 5½" (14cm) strip of white duct tape, folding it to shorten and match the length as you press it down against the white tape.//

Be sure to attach the Blue Plate duct tape to only half of the white duct tape strip lengthwise, leaving the other half of the sticky side exposed.

8 //H Place a circle sticker on the worktable, the parchment paper side facing down. Place the strip of ruffles around the perimeter of the circle sticker, the sticky half of the white duct tape strip facing down.//

9 TO MAKE THE MEDIUM-SIZE RUFFLES, place the

3" (7.5cm) strip of white duct tape on the worktable in the vertical position, sticky side facing up. //I Attach one of the long ends of the 8" (20.5cm) double-sided strip of Blue Plate duct tape to half the length of the 3" (7.5cm) strip of white duct tape, folding it to shorten and match the length as you press it down against the white tape.//

Be sure to attach the Blue Plate duct tape to only half of the white duct tape strip lengthwise, leaving the other half of the sticky side exposed.

10 On the same circle sticker from step 8,

attach this strip of ruffles around the ¹¹⁄₁₆" (1.7cm) inner circle, the sticky side of the white duct tape strip facing down.

11 TO MAKE THE CENTER RUFFLE OF THE

FLOWER, //J loosely roll the 6" (15cm) double-sided strip of Blue Plate duct tape into a spiral. Tightly wrap a 2" (5cm) strip of white duct tape around one of the rolled-up long edges into a base with a short stem.//

The spiral should now resemble a rose. //K On the same circle sticker used in steps 8 and 10, use the awl to punch a hole in the center of the circle.//

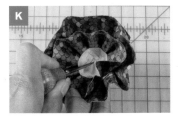

//L Push the stem of the rose through the hole. The flower is now complete.//

12 Repeat steps 5–11 until you have 16 completed

flowers attached to the circle stickers.

13 Starting from the top left and right corners of

one side of the bag, measure 1" (2.5cm) down along both the left and right edges and mark these points with a grease pencil. Using a ruler, draw a horizontal line connecting these 2 marks. Again from the top left and right corners of one side of the bag, measure 3" (7.5cm) down along the left and right edges and mark these points with a grease pencil. Using a ruler, draw a horizontal line connecting these marks. From the top left corner, measure 1" (2.5cm) inward along the top edge and mark this point. Draw a vertical line from this mark down to the bottom edge. From the top right corner, measure 1" (2.5cm) inward along the top edge and mark this point. Draw a vertical line from this mark to the bottom edge.

14 Repeat step 13 on the other 3 sides of the bag.

(continued on next page)

15 **//M** At all the points where the vertical lines intersect with the horizontal lines, use the awl to punch a hole through the fabric.**//**

There should be 16 holes.

16 Before placing a flower in each hole on the fabric, remove the parchment-paper backing from the circle sticker. **//N** Push the stem of the flower through the hole before pressing the sticker onto the bag fabric. On the inside of the bag, fold down the flower stems. Place 2 strips of 4" (10cm) white duct tape vertically on the inside of each bag side, covering the folded-down flower stems.**//**

17 **TO MAKE A STRAP,** cut a strip of 18" (45.5cm) white duct tape and place it on the worktable with the sticky side facing up. Fold the strip lengthwise into thirds.

18 Holding one end so the strap falls vertically, place it against the inside at the center of the bag opening, 2" (5cm) below the top edge. Place a 3" (7.5cm) strip vertically over the strap end, attaching it to the inside of the bag. Repeat this step using the other end of the strap and the opposite side of the bag opening.

A DIFFERENT TYPE OF GO BAG

"Go bags" are usually those duffle bags containing life's essentials that you would grab at a moment's notice. Impending doom on the horizon? You grab your go bag and run. But this little bag is shiny, fun, and ready for a night on the town. Carrying it around can feel like having your own personal disco ball, so you can bring a go-go dancing atmosphere to any party. This bag also has a chameleon's ability to match almost any outfit you wear, so you can just GO with it.

DUCT TAPE

white (heavy duty), 7 yd (6.4m)
silver glitter, 4 yd (3.7m)
black (heavy duty), 3 yd (2.7m)

ADDITIONAL MATERIALS

parchment paper, 15½" × 14½"
   (39.5cm × 37cm)
printout of 4" (10cm) equilateral
   triangle template (see page 201),
   trimmed to outline of shape
cardboard, at least 5" × 5" (12.5cm
   × 12.5cm)
2 neodymium magnets, ½" (13mm)
   diameter, ¹⁄₁₆" (1.5mm) thick

TOOLS

• scissors
• craft knife
• metal ruler
• graphite pencil
• black grease pencil

DIAGRAM 1

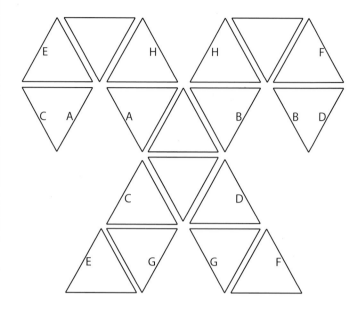

1 Place the parchment paper on the worktable in the portrait position and make a duct tape fabric (see page 10) using 9 strips of 15½" (39.5cm) white duct tape for the back side and 8 strips of 16½" (42cm) silver glitter tape for the front side.

2 //A Using a graphite pencil, trace the triangle template (page 201) on the cardboard and cut out the triangle. Discard the rest of the cardboard.//

3 //B Place the cardboard triangle on the white side of the duct tape fabric and trace with a grease pencil. Repeat 17 times until you have 18 triangles.//

Cut 18 triangles out of the duct tape fabric, discarding extra pieces.

4 //C Place the triangles on the worktable with the white duct tape side facing up. Assemble them into the formation in the diagram above.//

Cut 14 strips of 4" (10cm) white duct tape and cut them in half lengthwise. Place a strip over each seam between triangles to connect them in this formation. Save any extra white duct tape strips.

5 **TO MAKE THE MAIN POCKET OF THE BAG,**
//D using the extra white duct tape strips, connect the sides with the same letter (e.g., A to A, B to B, C to C, etc.).// Discard any extra tape strips.

6 **TO MAKE THE LIPS OF THE BAG,** cut 2 strips of 8" (20.5cm) black duct tape and fold them in half lengthwise.

7 **TO ATTACH THE LIPS TO THE BAG,** cut a strip of 8" (20.5cm) black duct tape in half lengthwise. //E Place a strip lengthwise along one long edge of each bag lip so that only half of each strip is attached to the lip.//

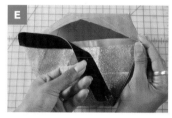

//F Line up the edge with the tape and the top edge of the bag opening and press the sticky side of the strip onto the inside of the bag.//

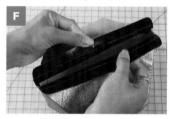

8 **TO MAKE THE STRAPS,** cut a strip of 24" (61cm) black duct tape in half lengthwise. Fold each strip into thirds.

9 Starting from the top left corner of the front bag lip, measure 1½" (3.8cm) inward

along the top edge and mark. Place 4" (10cm) of one end of a strap at the mark 1½" (3.8cm) below the top edge of the lip. //G Place a 5" (12.5cm) strip of black duct tape vertically over the strap end so it attaches to the inside of the bag.//

Repeat this step on the right side of the bag lip to attach the other end of the strap.

10 Flip the bag over and repeat step 9 to attach the second strap to the other bag lip.

11 Cut 2 strips of 3" (7.5cm) black duct tape and use them to center and attach the magnets to the inside of the bag lips (see page 14).

MANILA

The name of the bag refers to the capital of the Philippines, where my mother used to buy me these fantastic rattan purses. While I can't find a nice rattan-print duct tape, the white oak print does the trick, cut into jigsaw-like pieces and assembled against a black background. The Manila is meant to be the foil to a brightly colored outfit, the neutral tone that gives us permission to wear something more bold than we usually dare.

DUCT TAPE
black (heavy duty), 10 yd (9.1m)
white oak (Platypus brand), 4 yd (3.7m)

ADDITIONAL MATERIALS
parchment paper, 13" × 8" (33cm × 20.5cm)
parchment paper, 11½" × 4½"
    (29cm × 11.5cm)
printout of front/back and bottom templates (see
    pages 206–207), trimmed to outline of shape
printout of faux wood panels template
    (see page 206), trimmed to outline of shape
printout of spade template (see page 207),
    trimmed to outline of shape
4 neodymium magnets, ½" (13mm) diameter,
    1/16" (1.5mm) thick

TOOLS
• scissors
• craft knife
• metal ruler
• graphite pencil
• white grease pencil

1 For this project you will need 2 fabrics. Place the larger parchment paper on the worktable in the portrait position and make the first duct tape fabric (see page 10) using 8 strips of 9" (23cm) black duct tape for the back side and 5 strips of 14" (35.5cm) black duct tape for the front side. Repeat this step with the same parchment paper to make a second fabric. Set aside the parchment paper. (You will use it again in step 8.)

2 **TO MAKE THE FRONT PIECE OF THE BAG,** place one of the fabrics on the worktable in the landscape position. Place the front/back template in the center of the fabric. //A Use the white grease pencil to trace the outside shape onto the fabric. Cut out the shape from the fabric.// Discard any extra fabric.

3 **TO MAKE THE BACK PIECE OF THE BAG,** repeat step 2 with the second fabric.

4 To connect the front and back pieces, place them side by side on the worktable.

Align the bottom outer edges in between the two fabrics, creating a vertical middle seam. Starting at the bottom, place a 4½" (11.5cm) strip of black duct tape vertically over the seam, connecting the 2 fabrics. //**B** Starting at the bottom, place a 4½" (11.5cm) strip of black duct tape vertically on the left edge of the left fabric so that only half of the strip is on the fabric lengthwise.//

Fold back the tape strip so the sticky half faces up, and pull the right fabric to the left so that the left edge of the right fabric aligns with the left edge of the fabric below it. //**C** Press down along the left edge of both fabrics so the folded tape strip connects them. This is the main body of the bag.//

5 **TO MAKE THE BOTTOM PIECE,** place the smaller parchment paper on the worktable and make a duct tape fabric using 3 strips of

12½" (32cm) black duct tape for the back side and 7 strips of 5½" (14cm) black duct tape for the front side. Set aside the parchment paper. (You will reuse it in step 15.) //**D** Place the bottom bag template on the center of the fabric and trace it with a grease pencil.//

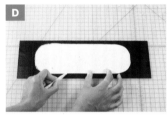

Cut out the shape from the fabric and discard any extra fabric.

6 //**E** Cut a 25½" (64.5cm) strip of black duct tape and attach it to the bottom edge of the main body of the bag, placing the tape on the back side so that half of the strip is exposed lengthwise and the sticky side is facing out.//

7 //**F** Align the perimeter of the bottom piece with the bottom edge of the main body and press the exposed tape strip against the back side of the bottom piece.//

8 **TO MAKE THE PANEL STICKERS,** place the faux wood panel template on the worktable. Place the left side of the larger parchment paper over the sticker template. Using a graphite pencil trace the entire template, then move the parchment paper over so the right side is over the sticker template. Do not move the template. Trace the entire template again. Be sure to use a sharpened pencil so the two sets of tracings match each other. Cut the parchment paper in half to separate the tracings. Cover the first tracing with 7 strips of 7½" (19cm) white-oak duct tape, placing the strips horizontally over the tracing, overlapping the long edges approximately ¼" (6mm) to form a connected piece.

9 Cover the second tracing with 4 strips of 12½" (32cm) white-oak duct tape. //**G** Place the strips vertically over the tracing, overlapping the long edges approximately ¼" (6mm) to form a connected piece.// Note that the grain print of the white-oak duct tape in this tracing is perpendicular to that of the first tracing.

G

10 //H With a pair of well-oiled scissors, cut out the panel stickers.//

H

//I Using the template as a guide, place the stickers on both the front and back of the bag.//

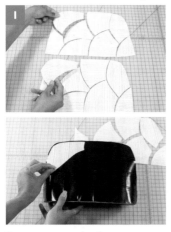

I

To accentuate the jigsaw element of the design, mix the pieces in the 2 sets.

11 TO MAKE THE STRAPS, cut 2 strips of 16" (40.5cm) black duct tape. Fold each one lengthwise into thirds.

12 Measure along the top edge at the bag opening to the center on both the front and back and mark with a white grease pencil. Measure 2¼" (5.5cm) to the left and right of center and mark these points. Measure straight down 1" (2.5cm) and mark these points. //J From these points, cut a 1" (2.5cm) horizontal slit toward the outer edges.//

J

13 //K On the front of the bag, insert 2" (5cm) of one end of one of the straps into the slit on the left side.//

K

Insert 2" (5cm) of the other end of the strap into the slit on the right side. On the inside of the bag, place a 3" (7.5cm) strip of black duct tape horizontally over each strap end to attach it to the bag.

14 Repeat step 13 on the back of the bag with the other strap.

15 TO MAKE THE SPADE STICKERS, on the smaller parchment paper, use a graphite pencil to trace the spade on the front/back template 4 times in a straight row. Cover the tracing with a strip of 8" (20.5cm) black duct tape. Flip the parchment paper over. With a pair of well-oiled scissors, cut out the spade stickers. Discard the parchment paper and extra tape.

16 Remove the parchment paper backing from the spade stickers. //L Place a sticker over each slit made in step 12 to cover the point of entry for the strap ends.//

L

17 Cut 2 strips of 7" (18cm) black duct tape to attach the 4 neodymium magnets (see page 14). Place a magnet on each tape strip end, approximately 1" (2.5cm) in from the ends. Place the tape strips horizontally on the inside of the front and back of the bag; the top edge of each strip should be approximately 1" (2.5cm) from the top edge of the opening.

ACKNOWLEDGMENTS

When you have a crazy passion, you need an agent who can see past the crazy and focus on the passion. Kate McKean: thank you for never giving up on duct tape—and me.

There is always a beginning and an end to a story worth telling. Caitlin Harpin and Emma Brodie: thank you for being at the beginning and end of my story.

When your own imagination is limited, you need a great art director, designer, and photographer to broaden your horizons. Stephanie Huntwork, Debbie Glasserman, and Sonia Persad, thank you for all the beauty and style that you brought to this book, and thank you also to Lauren Monchik who did a fantastic job putting it together. I would also like to thank Heather Williamson, Ada Yonenaka, Doris Cooper, Aaron Wehner, and the rest of my team at Clarkson Potter; I am humbled by your work and dedication—this is definitely *our* book. Stephanie Gonot: I weep when I think of how talented you are!

When your crazy passion keeps you up until 2 AM, you need a family who understands and loves you. Dave, Masana, and Mack: I love you forever.

And when your life gets twisted into a million knots, you need an editor who listens patiently to all your rants, all your non sequiturs, and all your "brilliant" ideas—and yet manages to keep you working toward your goal. Aliza Fogelson: you are my friend, and I thank you for saving me.

RESOURCES

A. I. Friedman
metal rulers, grease pencils, circles
inking templates, protractors
aifriedman.com
(800) 204-6352

Buckle Guy
o-rings, magnetic snap closures,
jeans buttons, grommet kits
buckleguy.com
(978) 213-9989

Dick Blick Art Materials
metal rulers, grease pencils, circles
inking templates, protractors
dickblick.com
(800) 828-4548

Duck Brand
duct tape
duckbrand.com
(800) 321-0253

Home Depot
magnets, grommet kits, awls, craft
knives, blades
homedepot.com
(866) 875-5488

Jo-Ann Fabric & Craft Store
duct tape, awls, craft knives,
scissors, metal rulers, graphite
pencils
joann.com
(888) 739-4120

K&J Magnetics
magnets
kjmagnetics.com
(888) 746-7556

Michaels
duct tape, awls, craft knifes,
scissors, metal rulers, graphite
pencils
michaels.com
(800) MICHAELS

Platypus Designer Duct Tape
duct tape
designerducttape.com
(919) 341-0420

Purse Supply Depot
o-rings, magnetic snap closures,
jeans buttons, grommet kits
pursesupplydepot.com
(909) 466-4777

3M Scotch Brand
duct tape
ducttape.scotchbrand.com
(800) 328-6276

Staples
duct tape, craft knives, scissors
staples.com
(800) 333-3330

Tape Brothers
duct tape
tapebrothers.com
(407) 260-0591

TEMPLATES

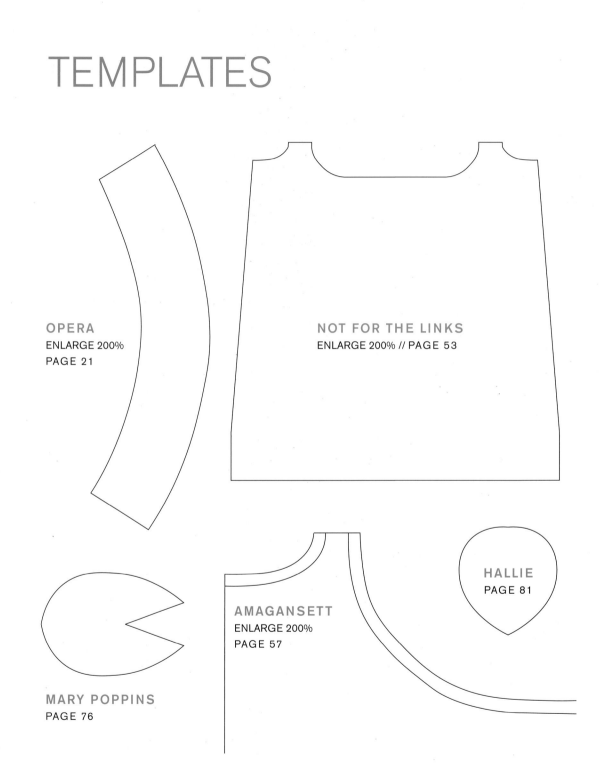

OPERA
ENLARGE 200%
PAGE 21

NOT FOR THE LINKS
ENLARGE 200% // PAGE 53

HALLIE
PAGE 81

AMAGANSETT
ENLARGE 200%
PAGE 57

MARY POPPINS
PAGE 76

REGATTA
ENLARGE 200% // PAGE 95

GRANNY SMITH
ENLARGE 200% // PAGE 44

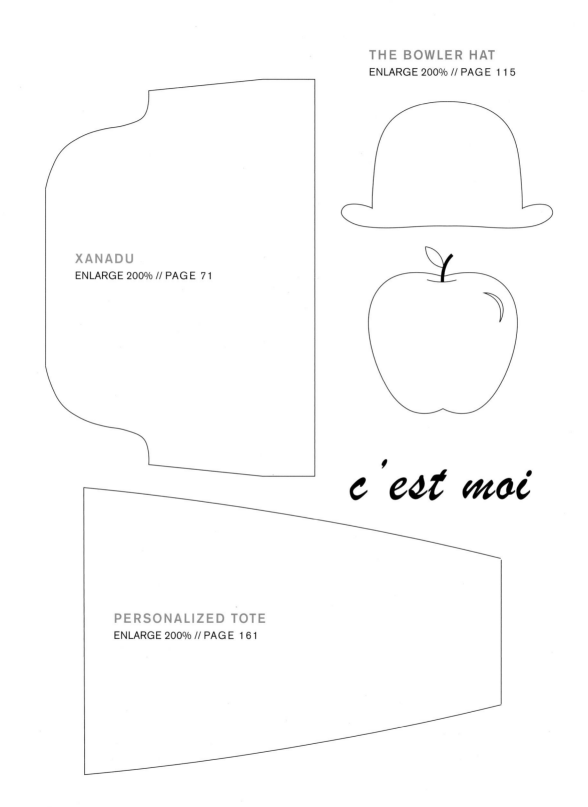

THE BOWLER HAT
ENLARGE 200% // PAGE 115

XANADU
ENLARGE 200% // PAGE 71

c'est moi

PERSONALIZED TOTE
ENLARGE 200% // PAGE 161

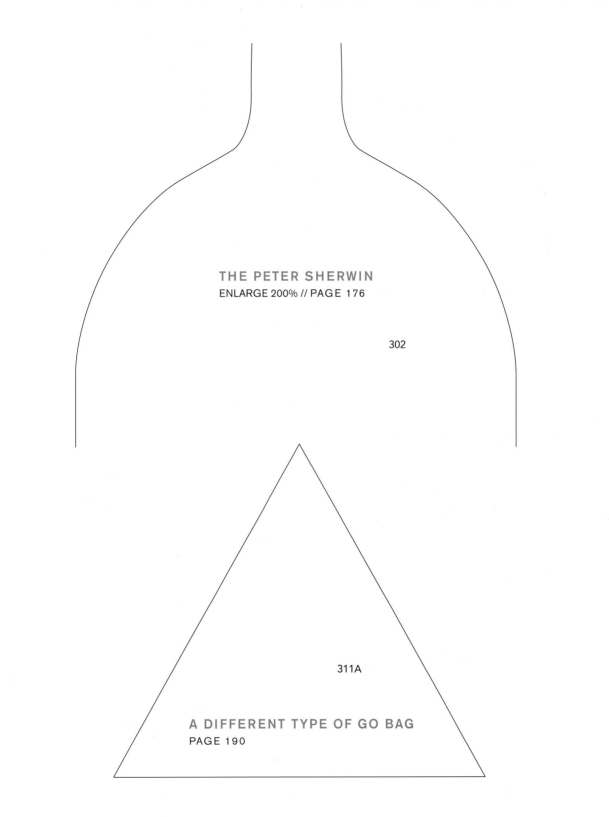

THE PETER SHERWIN
ENLARGE 200% // PAGE 176

302

311A

A DIFFERENT TYPE OF GO BAG
PAGE 190

SOBE 1 OF 2
ENLARGE 200%
PAGE 67

SOBE 2 OF 2
ENLARGE 200%
PAGE 67

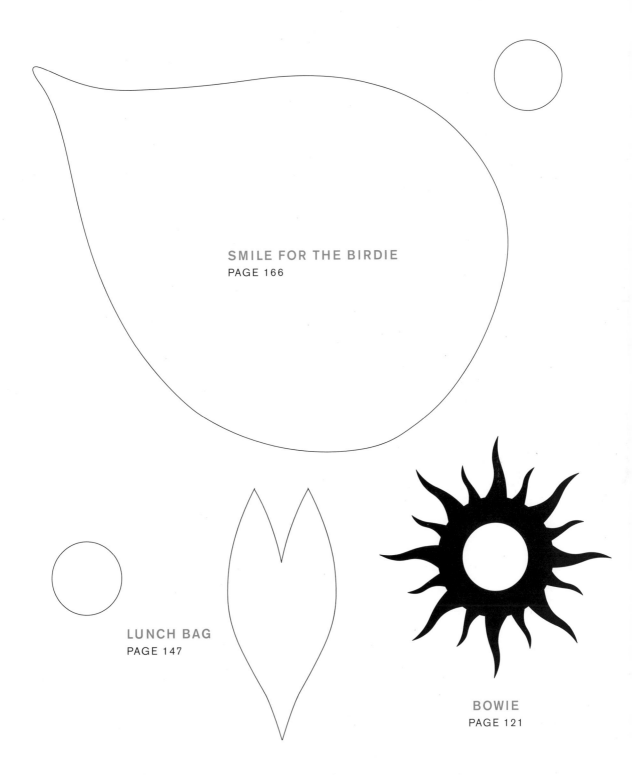

SMILE FOR THE BIRDIE
PAGE 166

LUNCH BAG
PAGE 147

BOWIE
PAGE 121

CARIBBEAN DREAM
ENLARGE 200%
PAGE 133

E.L.F.
ENLARGE 200%
PAGE 138

WHAM!
ENLARGE 200%
PAGE 125

261

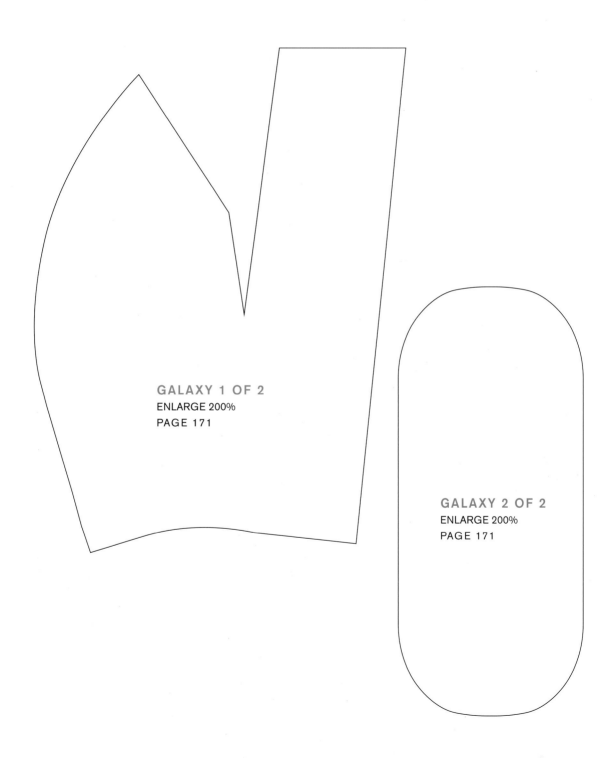

GALAXY 1 OF 2
ENLARGE 200%
PAGE 171

GALAXY 2 OF 2
ENLARGE 200%
PAGE 171

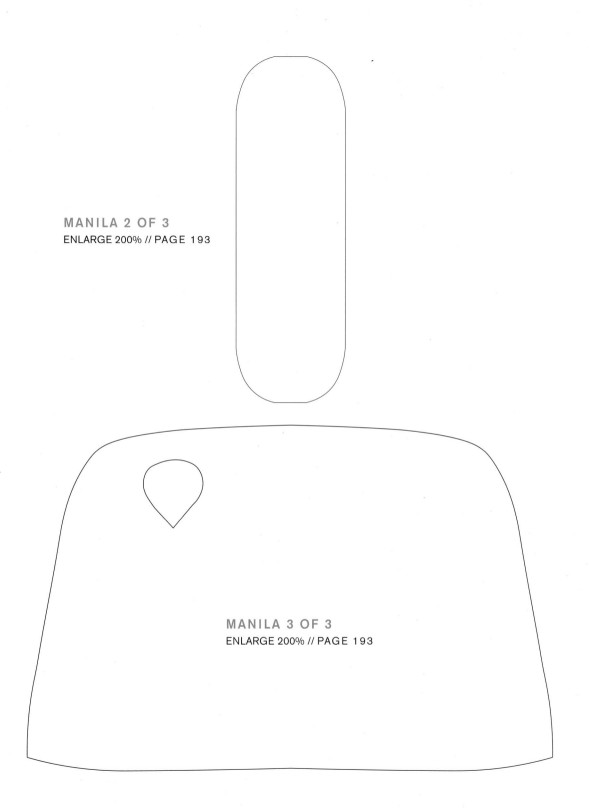

MANILA 2 OF 3
ENLARGE 200% // PAGE 193

MANILA 3 OF 3
ENLARGE 200% // PAGE 193

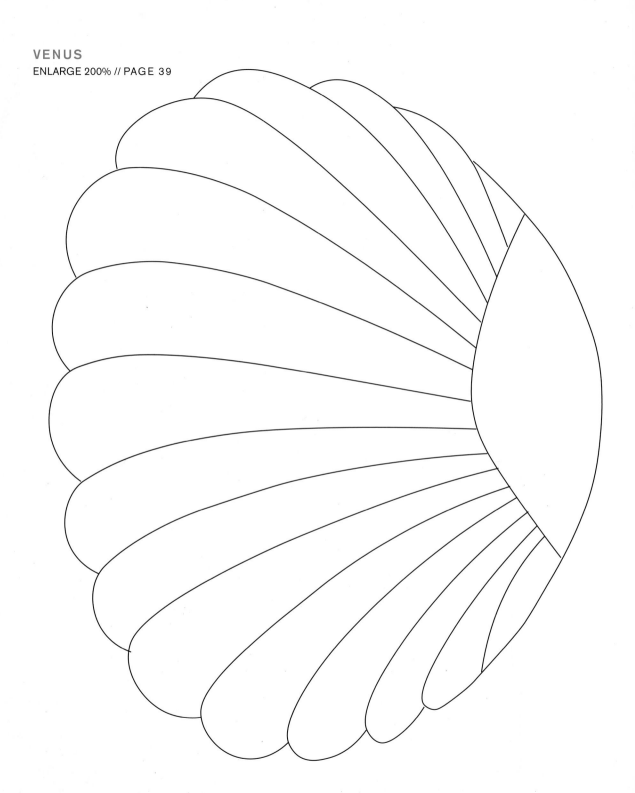